GINO'S ITALIAN EXPRESS
GINO D'ACAMPO

HODDER &
STOUGHTON

CONTENTS

INTRODUCTION

Once again I have been lucky enough to be given the chance to travel around Italy for a new TV series – this time by train. It was a fantastic journey that took in much of the north of Italy, including the cities of Turin, Siena, Pisa, Lucca, Florence, Bologna, Verona, Bolzano, Bergamo and Milan, as well as the Cinque Terre region on the Ligurian coast and the beautiful landscapes of Piedmont, Tuscany, the Dolomites and lakes Garda and Iseo. You can read about my routes and adventures in further detail on pages 8–16. Each journey was very different and amazing in its own way. I can definitely recommend them all and there is certainly a tour for everyone.

As I travelled around, I gathered recipes that were authentic, used local ingredients and for me evoked the places that I visited. Sometimes I adapted the recipes, either to give them my own twist, or to ensure the ingredients were widely available outside Italy. For instance, when I was in Piedmont I created an ice cream using Nutella – one of the region's most well-known products. In Cinque Terre, I made lemon tiramisù with limoncello, as an homage to the region's stunning, steep-sided hills, which are covered in lemon trees. I returned from Tuscany with a simple but excellent recipe for panforte, the rich, dense local fruit cake, and from Lombardy with a classic version of veal Milanese.

To reflect the express theme, I made sure I selected recipes that are quick and easy, while still being impressive and delicious. When conducting my research, I noticed that lots of 'quick' recipes were basic in flavour, so I made it my personal mission to create a book that offers you meals that I would serve at a dinner party, but that would not take long to prepare and cook. While some recipes require more time – for example, pizza dough needs to rise and ice cream has to freeze – they do not need a lot of hands-on time in the kitchen, giving you a chance to get on and do other things while you wait for your guests. Many of the recipes are now served on a monthly basis in my home.

There is a huge misconception that you need to spend hours in the kitchen to produce something special. I've proved in this book that this isn't the case. So for those of you who have busy lives and little time, yet who want to eat well and produce flavoursome Italian meals you can be proud of, I dedicate this book to you.

Ciao and *Buon Appetito*!

Gino xxx

GINO'S SCENIC TRAIN ROUTES

SWITZERLAND

Treno Dei Sapori (Lake Iseo)

Pisogne

Monte Isola

Peschiera Maraglio

Provaglio-Timoline

AUSTRIA

TRENTINO-ALTO ADIGE

Santa Maria Assunta

BOLZANO

Renon

SLOVENIA

FRIULI-VENEZIA GIULIA

Lake Garda

6

LOMBARDY

Pisogne

BERGAMO

8

MILAN

7

Treviglio

Brescia

Sirmione

Peschiera del Garda

VERONA

VENICE

VENETO

Gulf of Venice

Nogara

Mantua

5

Adriatic Sea

VAL D'AOSTA

TURIN

PIEDMONT

Alba

LIGURIA

GENOA

2

EMILIA-ROMAGNA

BOLOGNA

Treno Natura (Val d'Orcia)

SIENA

Asciano

Trequanda

CUNEO

1

Levanto

LA SPEZIA

LUCCA

Buonconvento

Torrenieri

FRANCE

Breil-sur-Roya

FLORENCE

Monte Antico

Monte Amiata

NICE

PISA

4

TUSCANY

SIENA

3

UMBRIA

Levanto

Cinque Terre Express

Monterosso

Varnazza

Corniglia

Manarola

Riomaggiore

LA SPEZIA

LAZIO

1. Tende Line
2. Cinque Terre Express
3. Treno Natura Line
4. Pisa-Lucca-Florence
5. Bologna-Verona

6. Garda-Bolzano
7. Milan-Bergamo
8. Bergamo-Lake Iseo
—— Gino's route
•••• Full train route

Ligurian Sea

NORTHERN ITALY BY TRAIN

Over the past few years I've spent a lot of time travelling around my beautiful homeland, mainly by car and boat. However, this time I was asked to take a tour of northern Italy by train for a new TV series and I jumped at the chance, as I hadn't been on a train for over 15 years.

There is something relaxing and exciting about travelling by train (and I'm not talking about the daily commute!). You can just sit back and admire the sights without the stress of driving and traffic jams, the rhythmic sounds of the engine can be soothing, there's plenty of space to walk around, you never know who you're going to meet, and, if you're lucky, there's a restaurant carriage – a big plus for me! Also, trains are better for the environment than planes and cars. I went on eight journeys in total and all were incredible in completely different ways – we travelled through spectacular mountain passes and rolling valleys and vineyards, alongside glistening lakes and sparkling coastlines, past pretty fishing villages and straight into major city centres. And of course, throughout my travels I sampled the typical foods of each area and enjoyed cooking for all the wonderful people I met. I learned so much from them, and it was a pleasure and an honour to be able to give something back.

THE FRENCH RIVIERA TO PIEDMONT

My first journey was travelling on the Tende Line, which starts in the French coastal city of Nice and ends in Italy's northwestern city of Turin five to six hours later. Taking in the French Riviera, the Alps and the stunning region of Piedmont, it is considered one of the most scenic train journeys in the world, and I give you my word it was *fantastico*!

We boarded the train in the French mountain town of Breil-sur-Roya. Carving a path through the Alps, we travelled through the village of Tende and on to the Italian border at Limone Piemonte, scaling 1000m above sea level, speeding over viaducts and passing picturesque vineyards and orchards bursting with fruit. A couple of hours later we reached the town of Cuneo – a spectacular city surrounded by the highest peaks and largest glaciers in Italy.

Piedmont is outstandingly beautiful, and it's also one of the most important wine-producing areas in Italy. There is an ancient tradition of winemaking here, dating back to Roman times, and the vineyards of Langhe-Roero and Monferrato, the hilly areas that surround the town of Alba, are a designated UNESCO World Heritage Site. Hazelnut groves are also abundant, and beautiful hilltop towns and villages dot the landscape. The region is home to two of my favourite things: Nutella, the world-famous hazelnut and chocolate spread, and Barolo, one of the world's greatest and oldest wines. In the past, locals worshipped Barolo (sometimes referred to as the 'king of wines') like a god with healing powers. To some extent this is still the case today. I met an interesting local hero, Doctor Roberto Alfonso, who often prescribes Barolo as a remedy to help illnesses. And I was surprised to see you can even buy Barolo in some churches!

Piedmont is also a foodie's paradise; there is a wealth of local delicacies, including white truffles, cured meats, artisan cheeses and a huge array of herbs. Making the most of the local produce, I prepared my simple but delicious No-bake chocolate and hazelnut cheesecake (see page 200) for Roberto and one of his patients. We enjoyed it overlooking the valley, relaxing and chatting with a glass of Barolo in hand. I really felt I was living *la dolce vita*!

Collecting my ticket for the final part of this journey, I headed to the metropolis of Turin – the first capital of Italy following the country's unification in 1861, until it was relocated to Florence in 1865 (Rome didn't serve as Italy's capital until 1871). Turin is also the town where the first Fiat car was born. Fiat is incredibly important to the Italian economy, and played a huge part in pulling Italy out of the recession at the end of World War II, helping to facilitate the reconstruction of the country and bringing prosperity to millions during this period. I was so excited when, on arrival at the station, I was greeted by three classic Fiat 500s in the colours of the cars featured in one of my favourite films, *The Italian Job*. I was then treated to a tour of the city Italian-Job style, recreating some of the film's most famous scenes. As if that wasn't enough, I was allowed to drive these wonderful cars on the rooftop test track of the Lingotto building, which Fiat built in the 1920s as their car factory (then the largest in Europe), fulfilling one of my lifelong dreams.

After all that excitement it was time for some relaxation, so I treated myself to the Turin speciality, *bicerin* – a soothing hot drink made of espresso and chocolate, topped with cream, and often served in a small glass. It is luxurious, rich and truly *bellissimo*!

THE ITALIAN RIVIERA: CINQUE TERRE

Continuing my journey in Italy's northwest, I headed to the spectacular, rugged stretch of the Italian Riviera known as the Cinque Terre (meaning 'five lands'). Situated on the Ligurian coast, the region consists of five spectacular small towns distinguished by their colourful painted houses built into the steep cliffs above the sea. The towns were once isolated fishing communities, accessible only by boat or on foot, but the advent of the railway, which links all the towns, transformed the lives of people living there, as well as making the area accessible for visitors.

It does not take long to travel from one end of the Cinque Terre to the other by train – about 20–30 minutes in total, with intervals of about four to six minutes between each station. However, most visitors want to disembark and walk around at least some of the towns, and it's fine to hop on and off the train at any or all of the stations en route. We set off on our trip from the nearby town of Levanto, stopping first at Monterosso, which is the largest and northernmost of the towns, with ancient castle ruins, tiny cobbled streets, main square and long beach.

We then travelled south to Corniglia, the smallest of the towns, where it was market day – a key part of life for the locals. There we met Eros and his father – two great characters who run a flower stall in the market. Eros is a local celebrity, renowned for bursting into song (usually opera) to draw in the customers. While I was lending a helping hand on the stall, I couldn't help but join in with the singsong – although, quite honestly, I'm not sure I really did much to encourage sales!

Our next stop was Manarola, one of the quieter towns, surrounded by terraced vineyards. There I met Giancarlo, who set up a local foundation after the terrible flash floods in 2011, to help to preserve the stone walls that prevent the town from falling into the sea. He took me on a trek up the mountain to see some of his work, and right there on the mountaintop I cooked my delicious *Minestra* (see page 62), to show appreciation for everything he and his colleagues have done and continue to do to preserve the town's fragile beauty.

Sadly, we had no time to visit Riomaggiore, but instead headed back north to Vernazza, often referred to as the most beautiful of the five towns, resembling a mini Portofino. With its enclosed natural harbour and houses grouped like an amphitheatre, this little town is enchanting, and understandably very popular. On arrival, I was met by Bartolo Lercari and his wife Lise, who took me on an incredible journey up the mountain on a monorail to visit their vineyard, where Bartolo's family have run the Cheo winery for 500 years, producing around 13,000 bottles of white wine a year. They run regular tasting sessions, and I sampled their very delicious dessert wine.

SIENA AND THE VAL D'ORCIA

The next leg of my journey took me to Tuscany, and if you're looking for stunning rural landscapes, spectacular architecture and top-notch art, it's hard to beat. My tour started in the beautiful medieval city of Siena, the location of the famous *Palio*. One of Italy's biggest sporting events, the *Palio di Siena* is a twice-yearly race that has taken place almost uninterruptedly since the mid-17th century at least, and involves ten horses and jockeys all riding bareback around the city's main square, the Piazza del Campo (sadly, not named after me!). The race lasts only 75 seconds on average, but the build up is immense. Local rivalries run deep, and the atmosphere is electric as two thirds of the city's population crowd into the square to witness the event.

In search of a sugar rush, I went to one of the oldest shops in Siena – the Antica Drogheria Manganelli – where I sampled the traditional Sienese snack known as *cavallucci* ('little horses'). Originating in Renaissance times, these chewy biscuits contain honey, candied fruit, nuts, aniseed and spices, including nutmeg and cinnamon. Today they are a popular Christmas treat.

I could have spent much longer exploring Siena, but the magnificent Tuscan countryside awaited me. In my opinion, there is no better way to see the landscape of this region than from the comfort of the *Treno Natura* steam train, with its carriages that date back to the early 1900s. Run by a group of retired Italian railwaymen, this heritage railway starts and ends in Siena, making a three-hour loop through the stunning landscape of the Val d'Orcia. The area directly south of the city, known as Crete Senesi, is considered by many to be the most beautiful part of Tuscany. Quite different from other parts of the region, it is characterised by sharp, steep-sided hills, which are greyish in colour due to the clay in the soil, giving an almost lunar appearance. Otherwise, the views on this route are classic Tuscany, with gently undulating hills, fields of wheat and sunflowers, rows of cypress trees, tiny hilltop villages and the odd isolated stone farmhouse.

The first main stop on this route is Monte Antico, where everyone gets off to watch the intriguing sight of the locomotive engine being moved from the back of the train and reattached to the front, so it faces the right way for the final ascent to the ancient hilltop town of Asciano. I was interested to learn that the town has its own version of the *Palio di Siena*, known as the *Palio dei Ciuchi*, in which competitors ride on donkeys. I spent the morning watching the riders train and tried to ride a donkey myself, but decided it might be best not to give up my day job! Instead, back in my comfort zone, I cooked panforte, a classic Tuscan fruit cake (see page 207). The locals say the recipe originated in Asciano – a claim hotly contested by the Sienese, who insist it was created in Siena. It is a centuries-old dispute that will no doubt continue for decades to come.

If you're keen on wine, there are countless tours of wineries around Siena, as it's the Chianti-producing region of Italy. I visited a family-run vineyard, Casa al Vento, where I indulged in some 'vinotherapy' – a spa treatment where the residues of winemaking (e.g. grape seeds and skins) are mixed with hot water and put in a large bathtub, along with a few bottles of red wine. Dating back to the Roman times, the treatment is said to be good for the skin and the soul. I must say, I felt very relaxed and rejuvenated afterwards, so there must be something in it.

PISA TO LUCCA AND FLORENCE

Continuing my tour of Tuscany I headed to Pisa, home of one of the world's most iconic buildings, the *Torre di Pisa*, as the Leaning Tower is known in Italy. The name 'Pisa' derives from the Greek word for marshy land, which the whole city is built on. Construction of the 58-metre marble bell tower (*campanile*) began in 1173 and finished in 1372, and as each storey was added on the tower leaned more and more. By the end of the 20th century the tower was leaning so much it was considered dangerous, so in 1990 a major straightening project was undertaken, which reduced the lean by 44cm. Today, engineers expect it to be stable for the next 200 years at least.

Having visited this amazing site, it was time to explore the rest of the city, and what better way to do this than to jump on a classic Vespa, whizzing around the streets and squares, and along the important 240km-long Arno river, which flows through both Florence and Pisa? Perhaps surprisingly, Pisa is not known for its food, but I guarantee you will not be disappointed if you find the Pizzeria Il Montino. It is famous for its *castagnaccio*, the most delicious chestnut cake you are ever likely to try. Satisfied after this sweet treat, I pulled up at the station for the next part of my journey, a 30-minute trip passing through the Tuscan countryside to the beautiful town of Lucca. Dividing the plain where the two cities are located is Monti Pisani – a range of low mountains, or hills. The area is most famous for its award-winning olive oil, but also for its chestnuts and mushrooms, which are included in many regional dishes. The area around Pisa and Lucca is also known for its asparagus, so in this book I've included several recipes containing this wonderful vegetable.

From Lucca it is a two-hour train journey through the stunning scenery of the Pistoia region to the jewel of Tuscany's crown – Florence. It is a place I have visited many times, but I am still blown away by its beauty, and there is so much to see. One of the more unusual things you can do in the city is to take part in *Cesarine*, where home cooks open their doors to the public. I co-hosted one with my new Florentine friend, Cecilia. She provided the venue and I prepared Chicken and pancetta cooked in beer (see page 123) for the guests. It went down a treat!

BOLOGNA TO VERONA

For many, the gastronomic heart of Italy is the Emilia-Romagna region. Its capital is Bologna, which is often overlooked by tourists but has a beautiful historic centre and a lively yet chilled-out atmosphere. Food has always been incredibly important here, and the cuisine is rich, containing plenty of cream and cheese. Outside Italy the city is best known for Bolognese sauce (*ragù*), but mortadella, the large Italian sausage, originates there too. Wine and socialising are also a key part of life in the city, and Bologna is home to what claims to be the world's oldest *osteria* (pub), Osteria del Sole, which dates back to 1465. In keeping with tradition, the bar serves only drinks, mainly wine, and the customers take their own food. Lambrusco is the traditional drink here and, trust me, it tastes so different from in the UK!

From Bologna we headed northwards by train, passing through Italy's main rice-growing region. Italy is Europe's largest rice producer, with most of it being grown in the lower, fertile and well-irrigated Po Valley plain. I visited a rice farm near Nogara in Veneto, where paddies stretch as far as the eye can see, then went to the nearby village of Villimpenta, to attend the Risotto Festival (*Festa del Risotto*) – a major event in the local calendar, which takes place in June. In fact, risotto festivals are held in a different nearby town or village each weekend all summer long. Risotto is such a popular dish in these parts, exceeding even pasta in popularity.

Just 30 kilometres north and a 10-minute train journey away is the exquisite city of Verona. Art student Gaia showed me around, ending at the 1st-century amphitheatre – the *pièce de résistance*. This striking piece of architecture is the largest open-air venue in Italy. Formerly used by gladiators, the venue now hosts operas and concerts throughout the summer.

LAKE GARDA TO THE DOLOMITES

From Verona it's a very short trip westwards to Lake Garda on one of Italy's high-speed trains, the *Frecciarossa*. In just over 10 minutes I made it to the town of Peschiera del Garda. The magnificent lake, which is visited by many millions of people per year, is right next to the station, providing breathtaking views the moment you arrive. From there, I headed west to the town of Sirmione. Situated at the end of the narrow peninsula, it provides incredible panoramic views of the lake. Each year, the local equivalent of the Venetian regatta is held here (the *Lega Bisse del Garda*) and is well worth a visit. I met the Sirmione rowing team, who gave me some tips on how to paddle and balance on the boat. As a thank you, I cooked them my hearty dish of Italian sausages and beans with garlic ciabatta (see page 143) by the side of the lake.

Returning to Verona, we boarded another train, which took us along Lake Garda high up into the mountains to Bolzano, also called Bozen. Considered one of the most scenic train journeys in Europe, the views en route to this town in Alto Adige (South Tyrol) are phenomenal. Bolzano is known as the Gateway to the Dolomites, and when you view the majestic, rugged mountain backdrop, you can see why. Despite Alto Adige being part of Italy, a quarter of the population speaks German as its first language, as the region was part of the Austrian-Hungarian Empire until World War I. I was met by Klaus, who runs a local folk dance troupe. Clad in lederhosen and dirndls, the group performs typical Tyrolean folk dances, slapping their thighs and the soles of their feet to the sounds of the accordion. (Of course, I couldn't resist joining in!) As well as the culture, the local cuisine is very Germanic. The bread is dark and seeded, and *wurstel* sausages (basically Frankfurters) are widely available.

In the main square of Bolzano you can catch the cable car up the mountain, where you then change to the Renon line (known in Italian as the *Ferrovia del Renon* and in German as the *Rittner Bahn*), which takes you high up into the Dolomites. It is a tiny, two-carriage light railway, which puffs up the mountain, climbing 1000 metres in about 20 minutes, until it reaches the Ritten plateau. Originally the line was created to link Bolzano to the villages located on the plateau, but today it is primarily for tourists and railway enthusiasts, and it starts higher up than it used to. The village at the end of the line, Santa Maria Assunta (also known as Maria Himmelfahrt) was popular in the 19th century with the people of Bolzano, who spent their weekends there, and the views are stunning. They love all things German in this village, particularly apple strudel. I decided to put my own Anglo-Italian spin on this dish and made them my Upside down apple crumble (see page 218), which went down a treat.

MILAN TO BERGAMO

My next tour began in Milan – the epitome of Italian fashion, with its high-end shops, bars and restaurants. The first thing I noticed was how stylish everyone looked – even the taxi drivers! There are some must-sees in the city, including the Duomo di Milano, the pink marbled cathedral that took 600 years to build, and the Galleria Vittorio Emanuele II, the world's oldest shopping mall. However, being in Milan is more about experiencing the atmosphere and enjoying the food and drink than intensive sightseeing.

Meeting up with friends for an *aperitivo* at the end of the working day is a key part of Milanese life, and I visited the fabulous and historic Bar Basso, which introduced this tradition to the Milanese. An *aperitivo* is basically a stiff pre-dinner drink (usually bitter-tasting such as Campari or Aperol), accompanied by bar snacks, as Italians never drink alcohol without eating.

As well as being sociable, this tradition is thought to whet the appetite for the main meal. Bar Basso is also known for its signature cocktail, *Negroni Sbagliato*, which was created there by accident when the barman, who was intending to make a Negroni, inadvertently added sparkling wine to Campari and vermouth instead of gin (*sbagliato* means 'bungled'). As I discovered on sampling the cocktail, this error was a blessing in disguise.

After exploring the city, I headed to the main train station, which is one of the largest in Europe and architecturally stunning. There I boarded a northbound train to Treviglio, home of the iconic Bianchi bike. I was lucky enough to take a tour of the factory and was lent an electric bike so I could explore the town on the many different cycle routes available.

My next stop was the beautiful city of Bergamo, about 40 kilometres northeast of Milan. The city is built on two distinct levels, which are linked by a funicular: the lower part (*Città Bassa*) is a busy modern town, while the upper section (*Città Alta*), built on a hill, is medieval and atmospheric. Surrounded by imposing Venetian walls, the old city contains a maze of winding cobblestone alleyways, cloisters and magnificent monuments, including the cathedral and basilica. Bergamo is known for its ice cream, and I visited the ice cream parlour where the famous *stracciatella* was created. There are all sorts of interesting places to visit in Bergamo, and I highly recommend a visit if you get the chance.

BERGAMO TO LAKE ISEO

My final destination was Lake Iseo, which I reached by train from Bergamo. Sandwiched between the two big tourist attractions, Lake Como and Lake Garda, Lake Iseo is often overlooked by many visitors, but locals refer to it as the true hidden gem of Italy and I must say I couldn't agree more. I was booked to serve food on the *Treno dei Sapori* (meaning 'train of flavours'), which transports tourists on a scenic route along the lake, and I was really looking forward to this new experience.

Of course, given we were at a lake it made sense for me to serve fresh fish, and fortunately Pietro, who comes from a long line of fishermen, was there to help. Along with some other members of his family, we boarded his boat and sailed out to the most favourable spot for sardine fishing, set up the catch nets and left them out overnight. It was amazing to return to the nets the following morning and discover them full of beautiful fishy treasures. I made my way back to the harbour with the catch, set up a makeshift kitchen and cooked the sardines then and there – right by the lake (see Grilled sardines with tomato and basil salad, page 52).

In the centre of the lake lies Monte Isola, the largest inhabited island in Europe. I was taken there by boat, with Andrea as my oarsman. Andrea is a renowned boat builder, whose family firm, Archetti Ercole, has been building wooden boats on the island since 1600 – so, trust me, there were plenty of stories. Cars are banned on the island, except for those of local dignitaries, such as the mayor (whom I met). The main town, Peschiera Maraglio, is charming, with winding streets and pretty pastel-coloured houses.

So my wonderful tour of northern Italy came to an end in Lombardy, almost 800 kilometres from my home in the south. The entire trip had been an absolute pleasure – the scenery was fantastic, the people were incredible, and the food was out of this world. And for me, touring around Italy by train was a great new experience and a real discovery. There is a saying, 'It's not about the destination, it's about the journey' – for me, in the context of my tour of Italy, it's about both. I cannot recommend it highly enough – and now it's time for you to get booking!

GINO'S EXPRESS COOK KIT

Throughout this book I mention the equipment I use for each recipe. If you follow this it will make preparation of ingredients and cooking easier and will save you time. Below is a list of what I have in my cook kit. If you don't have exactly the right piece of equipment for the recipe, don't worry. You can often improvise or substitute one item for another.

POTS AND PANS

I regularly use three deep saucepans and three frying pans of differing sizes, one shallow saucepan, a flameproof casserole and a cast-iron chargrill pan.

SAUCEPANS

Small saucepan: 16–19cm diameter and 8–10cm deep
Medium saucepan: 20–21cm diameter and 10–12cm deep
Large saucepan: 22–25cm diameter and 12–15cm deep
Large shallow saucepan/sauté pan: 26–28cm diameter and 8cm deep

FRYING PANS

Small frying pan: 20–21cm diameter
Medium frying pan: 24–26cm diameter
Large frying pan: 26–32cm diameter

FLAMEPROOF CASSEROLE

Made of cast iron, this retains heat well and can be used on the hob or in the oven.

CAST-IRON CHARGRILL PAN

Gives food a grilled flavour and attractive markings, but a frying pan or grill can be used instead. I often use it for toasting ciabatta.

OVENWARE

I have a range of different-sized tins for baking and roasting. Most are metal (it is the best conductor of heat), but I also use ceramic baking dishes for *al forno* recipes.

BAKING SHEET/TRAY

Flat or shallow metal trays are good for baking pizza, biscuits and other small items; they can also be used under the grill.

TRAYBAKE TIN

A deeper tin used for pizzas that are cut into squares before serving.

ROASTING TIN

A metal tin, often with deeper sides, which is ideal for roasting vegetables and meat.

BAKING DISH

Made of ceramic, stoneware or heatproof glass, baking dishes are ideal for baked pasta dishes such as lasagne or cannelloni. You can put them under the grill but not on the hob.

RAMEKIN

Available in various different sizes, ramekins are small ceramic baking dishes, ideal for individual portions, particularly soufflés.

CAKE TINS

I have several cake tins, but the one I use most is 23cm diameter and 8cm deep, with a loose base for easy removal. For more delicate cakes, such as cheesecake, I use a springform tin, as you can remove the sides without damaging the cake.

BOWLS, CONTAINERS AND PLATTERS

Whatever you're preparing, you need a good selection of bowls and dishes for a variety of different tasks.

MIXING BOWLS

I regularly use a selection of different-sized mixing bowls, ranging from small (12–16cm) to medium (16–20cm) and large (20–25cm).

HEATPROOF BOWL

A heatproof bowl, set over a pan of simmering water, is useful for melting chocolate.

FREEZERPROOF CONTAINER

A rigid plastic container with a lid is useful for making and storing ice cream and sorbets.

SERVING PLATTERS

When entertaining, I like to use large serving platters for antipasti and salads; they look fantastic and make eating a shared, informal, sociable experience. My favourite is oval and about 40 x 30cm.

TOOLS AND UTENSILS

There is a huge array of kitchen utensils and gadgets available, many of which are not essential. Here is a list of those that I use regularly.

Blenders (hand-held and freestanding)
Chopping boards
Colander
Food processor
Garlic crusher
Graters (microplane and box grater)
Knives (a selection for different tasks)
Ladle
Lemon squeezer
Measuring jug
Measuring spoons
Meat mallet
Pastry brush
Sieve
Slotted spoon
Spatula (flexible and wooden)
Timer
Tongs
Vegetable peeler
Weighing scales
Whisks (electric and hand)
Wooden spoons

CONVERSION TABLES

These are approximate conversions, which have been rounded up or down. Never mix metric and imperial measures in one recipe.

WEIGHTS

25g	1oz
50g	2oz
100g	3½oz
150g	5oz
200g	7oz
250g	9oz
300g	10oz
400g	14oz
500g	1lb 2oz
1kg	2¼lb

VOLUME (LIQUIDS)

5ml		1 tsp
15ml		1 tbsp
30ml	1 fl oz	⅛ cup
60ml	2 fl oz	¼ cup
75ml		⅓ cup
120ml	4 fl oz	½ cup
150ml	5 fl oz	⅔ cup
175ml		¾ cup
250ml	8 fl oz	1 cup
1 litre	1 quart	4 cups

LENGTHS

1cm	½ inch
2.5cm	1 inch
20cm	8 inches
25cm	10 inches
30cm	12 inches
35cm	14 inches

OVEN TEMPERATURES

140°C	275°F
150°C	300°F
160°C	325°F
180°C	350°F
190°C	375°F
200°C	400°F
220°C	425°F
230°C	450°F

VOLUME (DRY INGREDIENTS – AN APPROXIMATE GUIDE)

butter	225g	1 cup
flour	125g	1 cup
sugar	200g	1 cup
breadcrumbs (fresh)	50g	1 cup
nuts (e.g. almonds)	125g	1 cup
dried fruit (raisins, mixed peel)	150g	1 cup
grains and small dried legumes	200g	1 cup
grated cheese	100g	1 cup

ANTIPASTI & SOUPS

ANTIPASTI & SOUP

RECItES

ITALIAN-STYLE SPICY ROASTED NUTS *NOCCIOLINE PICCANTI*

Clearly this is not a proper starter, but I've made this recipe on many occasions to get the party started, as these spicy nibbles are the perfect accompaniment to an *aperitivo*. They're also great to serve at a barbecue, so guests can nibble on something while waiting for their food. If you have any left over, you can keep them in an airtight container for up to 10 days.

1 Preheat the oven to 200°C/gas mark 6. Put the chilli powder, garlic powder, rosemary, salt and pepper in a medium bowl. Pour over the oil and 2 tablespoons of water and stir to make a paste.

2 Add the nuts and mix well to combine, ensuring they are evenly coated in the oil and flavourings.

3 Tip the nuts onto a baking sheet and spread them out evenly. Roast for 8 minutes then remove from the oven and stir the nuts around. Return to the oven for a further 2 minutes. Leave to cool.

Serves 12

3 teaspoons hot chilli powder
1 teaspoon garlic powder
2 tablespoons chopped fresh rosemary
2 teaspoons fine salt
1 teaspoon ground black pepper
3 tablespoons extra virgin olive oil
120g whole raw cashew nuts (unsalted)
120g whole raw hazelnuts
120g walnut halves
120g whole unblanched almonds

BRUSCHETTA WITH CHERRY TOMATOES AND ANCHOVIES *BRUSCHETTA CON POMODORI E ACCIUGHE*

I first tasted bruschetta with anchovies while filming on the Ligurian coast. The locals love these salty little fish, and they combine wonderfully with tomatoes to make an intensely flavoured, piquant topping. If you don't have ciabatta, it's fine to use any crusty, country-style bread. Serve these bruschette on their own, with chilled white wine, or together with other antipasti.

1 Place the tomatoes and anchovies in a medium bowl and season with salt and pepper. Pour over the oil, add the parsley and stir to combine. Set aside.

2 Preheat a ridged cast-iron chargrill pan over a high heat for 5–10 minutes. Meanwhile, brush a little oil over both sides of the ciabatta.

3 When the pan is very hot, place the ciabatta in the pan and grill for 1–2 minutes each side or until golden brown. Transfer to a plate or board. Rub the garlic clove over both sides of the toasts.

4 Top the toasts with the tomato and anchovy mixture.

Serves 4

15 fresh red cherry tomatoes, quartered
15 fresh yellow cherry tomatoes, quartered
50g anchovy fillets in oil, drained and finely chopped
4 tablespoons extra virgin olive oil, plus extra for brushing
2 tablespoons chopped fresh flat-leaf parsley
8 slices of ciabatta, about 2cm thick
1 garlic clove, peeled
Salt and freshly ground black pepper

BRUSCHETTA WITH GORGONZOLA, PARMA HAM AND HONEY *BRUSCHETTA CON GORGONZOLA, PROSCIUTTO CRUDO E MIELE*

In Milan you'll find Gorgonzola served in a multitude of ways. Traditionally from Lombardy, the cheese takes its name from a small town (now a suburb of Milan), where it is thought to have originated in the 12th century. In this recipe I love how the salty Gorgonzola and Parma ham contrast with the sweetness of the honey. If you don't have Gorgonzola, you can use any other blue cheese.

1 Preheat a ridged cast-iron chargrill pan over a high heat for 5–10 minutes. Meanwhile, brush a little of the oil over both sides of the ciabatta.

2 Lay the ciabatta in the pan and grill for 1–2 minutes each side or until golden brown. Transfer to a plate or board. Rub the garlic clove over both sides of the toasts.

3 Spread the Gorgonzola evenly over one side of the toasts. Arrange a slice of Parma ham on top and drizzle over the honey.

Serves 4

Olive oil for brushing
8 slices of ciabatta, about 2cm thick
1 garlic clove, peeled
150g Gorgonzola cheese (room temperature)
8 slices Parma ham
8 teaspoons runny honey

CAPRESE SALAD *INSALATA CAPRESE*

No matter where you are in Italy, the Caprese salad (which originates in southern Italy) is more often than not featured on menus and served at parties and special occasions. The combination of tomatoes, garlic and mozzarella is just perfect, and the salad looks so beautiful. Always use the best-quality tomatoes, in season. The good news for vegetarians is that rennet-free buffalo mozzarella is now available in many Italian delis and supermarkets. Serve with warm crusty bread or my Cheesy ciabatta (see page 62).

1 Place the tomatoes in a medium bowl with the basil and garlic. Season with salt and pepper. Pour over the oil and stir to combine. Leave for 10 minutes at room temperature, stirring occasionally.

2 Carefully spoon the tomatoes onto 4 plates, reserving the juices in the bowl.

3 Using a tablespoon, make a small hollow in the centre of the tomatoes. Place one ball of mozzarella in each 'nest'. Using a sharp knife, make a cross cut in the mozzarella, about 1cm deep. Gently open out the cheese and place 1 basil leaf inside. Drizzle over 1 tablespoon of the reserved juices.

Serves 4

5 large ripe fresh plum tomatoes, cut into chunks
15 fresh red cherry tomatoes, halved
15 fresh yellow cherry tomatoes, halved
10 fresh basil leaves, plus 4 leaves to garnish
2 garlic cloves, peeled and finely chopped
8 tablespoons extra virgin olive oil
4 x 125g balls of buffalo mozzarella cheese, drained
Salt and freshly ground black pepper

TUNA AND BEAN SALAD *TONNO E FAGIOLI*

Each year I spend the summer with my family on the island of Sardinia, and we enjoy this salad at least once a week. My wife often makes it in the morning and stores it in a sealed plastic container in the fridge, in preparation for our boat trips. Sometimes she adds a few sun-dried tomatoes or pickled onions – to be honest, you can add pretty much whatever you fancy. Buy tuna in oil rather than in brine, which has the texture of cat food! Serve with warm crusty bread.

1 Put the beans in a large bowl. Add the olives, tomatoes, onion and chives. Season with salt and pepper.

2 Pour over the oil and mix all the ingredients together. Set aside for about 5 minutes to allow the flavours to combine.

3 Just before serving, add the tuna and mix gently, trying not to break up the chunks too much.

Serves 4

1 x 400g tin of cannellini beans, rinsed and drained
1 x 400g tin of butter beans, rinsed and drained
100g pitted green olives, drained and halved
10 fresh red cherry tomatoes, quartered
10 fresh yellow cherry tomatoes, quartered
1 large red onion, peeled and finely sliced
3 tablespoons chopped fresh chives
6 tablespoons extra virgin olive oil
480g tuna chunks in oil (tinned or in a jar), drained
Salt and freshly ground black pepper

CHICKEN LIVER PÂTÉ WITH TOASTED GARLIC CIABATTA *CROSTINI CON PATÈ DI FEGATINI*

This is a really quick yet luxurious first course, perfect for entertaining. It does require chilling time, but you can make it in the morning, then forget about it. This recipe is one of the top-selling dishes in my restaurants, and we usually serve it with grissini breadsticks. You can use orange marmalade instead of strawberry jam if you prefer. *Buon Appetito*!

1 Heat 2 tablespoons of the oil in a medium frying pan over a medium heat. Add the chicken livers and fry for 6–8 minutes or until cooked through, stirring continuously. Remove with a slotted spoon and transfer to a food processor.

2 Add the remaining 2 tablespoons of oil to the same pan. Add the shallots and rosemary and fry for about 3 minutes.

3 Increase the heat to high. Pour in the brandy and let it bubble for 30 seconds. Stir and scrape the bottom of the pan to release any sticky bits left from the chicken livers.

4 Transfer the mixture, including the juices, to the food processor. Add the honey, jam and half the butter. Season with salt and pepper. Blitz to a smooth paste.

5 Spoon the mixture into 4 small ramekins, about 9cm diameter and 5cm high. Melt the remaining butter and pour over the top. Cover with cling film and chill for 3 hours.

6 About 20 minutes before you are ready to serve, remove the pâté from the fridge. Meanwhile, toast the ciabatta on both sides until golden brown. Rub the garlic clove over both sides of the toasts. Serve alongside the pâté.

Serves 4

4 tablespoons extra virgin olive oil
400g chicken livers, trimmed
4 shallots, peeled and chopped
1 tablespoon chopped fresh rosemary
4 tablespoons brandy
1 tablespoon runny honey
1 tablespoon good-quality strawberry jam
200g salted butter (room temperature)
8 slices of ciabatta, about 1cm thick
1 garlic clove, peeled
Salt and freshly ground black pepper

DEEP-FRIED MOZZARELLA SANDWICH *MOZZARELLA IN CARROZZA*

This was my late father Ciro's favourite starter/snack. He was always so happy when my mother made it for him. The Italian name translates as 'mozzarella in a carriage', and mozzarella is really the only essential ingredient for the filling – the rest is up to you. Try adding anchovies, salami, sun-dried tomatoes, cooked ham or a teaspoon of black olive paste … you can pretty much add whatever you like. I hope you enjoy these little treats as much as Papa did!

1 Cut each mozzarella ball into 4 slices. Lay a double layer of kitchen paper on a large plate and place the mozzarella on top. Cover with another double layer of kitchen paper. Press firmly to extract any excess milk from the mozzarella. Set aside.

2 Put the flour on a large plate. Spread out the breadcrumbs on another plate. Beat the eggs in a large bowl with the milk and some salt and pepper. Set aside.

3 Using a rolling pin or the palm of your hand, press down each bread slice until flat.

4 Place 1 slice of mozzarella on 1 half of each slice of bread and top with a basil leaf. Fold over the bread to cover the mozzarella and make a rectangle. Gently press down with your palm. Dip the edges of the bread in the egg. Using your fingertips, press down the edges firmly to seal.

5 Use one hand to dip each sandwich in the flour (shake off the excess), then the eggs (let excess drain back into the dish) then transfer to the plate with the breadcrumbs. Use your other hand to coat the sandwich evenly with the breadcrumbs, patting them firmly into the egg so they stick.

6 Heat the oil in a large shallow saucepan until very hot. To check if the oil is ready, sprinkle in a few breadcrumbs; they will sizzle when the oil is hot enough for frying.

7 Fry the sandwiches in 2 batches for about 2 minutes each side or until golden brown. Remove with a slotted spoon and drain on kitchen paper. Season with salt and pepper and serve immediately.

Serves 4

2 x 125g balls of buffalo mozzarella cheese, drained
100g plain flour
150g dried fine breadcrumbs
3 medium eggs
2 tablespoons full-fat milk
8 slices of white bread, crusts removed
8 large fresh basil leaves
About 600ml vegetable or sunflower oil for deep-frying
Salt and freshly ground black pepper

GRILLED STUFFED AVOCADO *AVOCADO GRIGLIATO RIPIENO*

I had never seen an avocado until I came to London in 1994. They just weren't a feature of southern Italian cuisine. However, since I have been travelling around Italy for the TV series, I realise they are actually very common in northern Italy, featuring on lots of restaurant menus. This grilled stuffed avocado recipe is great when you want something healthy but filling. I normally eat two halves, but one half is certainly enough for a starter portion.

1 Preheat the grill to its highest setting. Brush the avocado flesh with a little oil and grill, flesh-side up, for about 3 minutes or until starting to brown. Set aside.

2 Put the tomato, olives and spring onions in a medium bowl. Add the oil and vinegar. Season with salt and pepper and stir to combine.

3 Carefully spoon the filling into the avocados. Place a slice of mozzarella on top of each.

4 Return the avocados to the grill and cook for about 3 minutes or until the mozzarella starts to melt. Serve immediately.

Serves 4

2 large ripe avocados, halved and stoned
2 tablespoons extra virgin olive oil, plus extra for brushing
1 large fresh plum tomato, deseeded and cut into 1cm chunks
60g pitted green olives, drained and roughly chopped
2 spring onions, trimmed and roughly chopped
1 tablespoon balsamic vinegar
1 x 125g ball of mozzarella cheese, drained and cut into 4 slices
Salt and freshly ground black pepper

GRILLED ASPARAGUS WITH A POACHED EGG *ASPARAGI GRIGLIATI CON UOVA IN CAMICIA*

I cooked this recipe when I was filming in the beautiful Tuscan town of Lucca, where I met a violin maker called Fabio. He told me all about how to make the perfect violin and how long it takes – 240 hours of really hard work. To say thank you for the wonderful day we spent together, I cooked him asparagus, his favourite vegetable, with a poached egg – a classic combination. If you prefer, you can boil or steam the asparagus instead of grilling.

1 Heat a ridged cast-iron chargrill pan over a high heat for 5 minutes. Meanwhile, put the asparagus on a plate and drizzle over 2 tablespoons of the oil. When the pan is very hot, lay the asparagus in the pan and grill for about 5 minutes or until tender but still firm (al dente), turning occasionally.

2 Meanwhile, prepare the poached eggs. Place a medium saucepan filled with 2.5 litres of hot water over a high heat. Stir in the vinegar and some salt. Bring to the boil then reduce the heat to a gentle simmer.

3 Poach the eggs in 2 batches. Break one egg into a cup. Slowly slide it into the water. Repeat for the second egg, keeping it well apart from the first so the eggs are not touching each other.

4 Poach very gently for 3–4 minutes or until the white is set. Keep the water at a very gentle simmer throughout to ensure the eggs do not become too hard; you just want a few bubbles breaking the surface. Using a slotted spoon, lift out the eggs and transfer to a plate or kitchen paper to drain. Repeat for the remaining eggs.

5 Divide the asparagus between warm plates and carefully place 1 poached egg on top of each serving. Season with a pinch of salt and pepper and drizzle over the remaining 4 tablespoons of oil.

Serves 4

300g fine asparagus, woody ends removed
6 tablespoons extra virgin olive oil
3 tablespoons white wine vinegar
4 very fresh eggs
Salt and freshly ground black pepper

GENOVESE MUSSELS WITH PESTO AND OLIVES *COZZE ALLA GENOVESE*

Mussels with pesto – it's not a combination that you see every day, but in Genoa it's really popular. To be honest, I wasn't sure about the idea before I tried it, but I soon changed my mind. The aromatic flavour of the basil and the saltiness of the mussels work really well together, the pine nuts add texture, and the Leccino olives add a subtle piquancy – simply *fantastico*! Make sure you buy the best-quality olives and pesto, as they're vital for the success of this dish. Serve with warm crusty bread.

1 Scrub the mussels under cold running water. Rinse away the grit and remove barnacles with a small, sharp knife. Remove the 'beards' by pulling the dark, stringy piece away from the mussels. Discard any open mussels or mussels with broken shells. Set aside.

2 Heat the oil in a large saucepan over a medium heat. Add the garlic and olives and as soon as the garlic starts to sizzle, add the mussels. Cook for about 2 minutes, stirring continuously. Increase the heat to high, add the wine and simmer for about 3 minutes, stirring occasionally.

3 Cover the saucepan and cook for a further 3 minutes or until the mussels start to open, shaking the pan occasionally.

4 Add the tomatoes, basil and pesto and season with salt and pepper. Stir to combine and cook for about 5 minutes, uncovered, stirring occasionally.

5 Discard any mussels that have not opened. Ladle into warm bowls and serve immediately.

Serves 4

1.2kg live mussels
4 tablespoons extra virgin olive oil
4 garlic cloves, peeled and sliced
100g pitted black olives (preferably Leccino or Kalamata), drained
150ml dry white wine
20 fresh red cherry tomatoes, halved
10 large fresh basil leaves
3 tablespoons good-quality, shop-bought basil pesto
Salt and freshly ground black pepper

SPICY PRAWNS WITH A TUNA AND CAPER SAUCE *GAMBERONE PICCANTE TONNATO*

Tuna sauce is an Italian classic from Piedmont, usually served with veal in the dish *Vitello tonnato*. A few years ago, I adapted the recipe with prawns and it was a big hit – the spicy garlic prawns perfectly complement the creamy, piquant sauce. You can prepare the sauce ahead; just cover and refrigerate it until you're ready to fry the prawns.

1 First make the sauce. Put the tuna, anchovies, mayonnaise, capers and oil in a blender. Blitz until smooth.

2 Transfer the mixture to a small bowl and stir in the parsley. The consistency of the sauce should be like thick double cream; if necessary, stir in a little cold water to make the sauce slightly runnier. Set aside.

3 Place a medium frying pan over a high heat. Add the butter, oil, garlic and chilli flakes. As soon as the garlic starts to sizzle, fry the prawns for about 1 minute each side or until pink. Season with salt.

4 To serve, divide the sauce among 4 plates, creating a circle about 10cm in diameter. Arrange the prawns on top, slightly overlapping, and drizzle over any juices from the pan. Scatter over the capers and serve immediately.

Serves 4

60g salted butter
2 tablespoons extra virgin olive oil
2 large garlic cloves, peeled and thinly sliced
1 teaspoon dried chilli flakes
20 raw, peeled large king prawns, deveined
1 tablespoon capers, drained
Salt

For the sauce
320g tuna chunks in olive oil (tinned or in a jar), drained
4 anchovy fillets in oil, drained
200g mayonnaise
1 tablespoon capers, drained
2 tablespoons extra virgin olive oil
2 tablespoons chopped fresh flat-leaf parsley

GRILLED SARDINES WITH TOMATO AND BASIL SALAD *SARDINE ALLA GRIGLIA CON INSALATA DI POMODORINI E BASILICO*

When I was filming on Lake Iseo, I was asked to serve passengers on the *Treno dei Sapori*, the tourist train that travels along the lake. Given the lake is full of fish, I decided to catch my own sardines, then I grilled them by the side of the lake. It was tricky plating up and serving the sardines and tomato salad on a moving train, but the customers seemed happy with the results! This dish can also be served as a main course, in which case allow four sardines per person.

1 Place the sardines in a non-metallic rectangular dish and make the marinade. Put the oil, garlic, capers, chilli powder and fennel seeds in the dish with the sardines. Season with salt. Squeeze over the juice of the lemon. Roughly tear the spent shells and add the pieces to the marinade. Carefully toss the sardines in the marinade, cover and chill for at least 30 minutes.

2 Meanwhile, make the salad. Put the tomatoes in a medium bowl. Add the garlic and tear over the basil leaves. Season with salt and drizzle over the oil. Gently stir to coat the tomatoes in the oil and set aside.

3 About 10 minutes before cooking, remove the sardines from the fridge. Place a ridged chargrill pan over a medium heat for 5–10 minutes.

4 When the pan is very hot, carefully lift the sardines out of the marinade and place them in the pan. Add the lemon shells from the marinade and discard the remaining marinade. Cook for 3 minutes then turn and cook for a further 2 minutes.

5 To serve, put 2 sardines on each plate and sprinkle over the parsley. Put the tomato salad alongside the fish. Garnish with a wedge of fresh lemon and a piece of the chargrilled shell.

Serves 4

8 whole sardines (about 60g each), scaled and gutted
4 tablespoons extra virgin olive oil
2 garlic cloves, peeled and sliced
1 tablespoon capers, drained
½ teaspoon chilli powder
1 teaspoon fennel seeds
1 large unwaxed lemon, plus 4 lemon wedges to serve
2 tablespoons chopped fresh flat-leaf parsley
Salt

For the salad
20 red baby plum tomatoes, halved
20 yellow baby plum tomatoes, halved
3 garlic cloves, peeled and sliced
20 fresh basil leaves
6 tablespoons extra virgin olive oil

CHARGRILLED POLENTA WITH CREAMY GARLIC MUSHROOMS *POLENTA GRIGLIATA CON FUNGHI CREMOSI*

Made from cornmeal, polenta is a traditional, staple food throughout northern Italy, where it is cooked in many different ways: simply boiled, fried or grilled. This recipe is incredibly quick and easy, and it is the ideal dish to make in autumn, when mushrooms are in season. If you can't find polenta, serve the creamy mushrooms on toasted ciabatta instead. Delicious!

1 Heat the butter and oil in a large frying pan over a high heat. Add the rosemary and mushrooms, season with salt and fry for 5 minutes, stirring occasionally. Add the garlic and fry for about 5 minutes.

2 Pour over the wine and boil for about 2 minutes. Reduce the heat to medium, stir in the cream and tomatoes and season with pepper. Simmer for about 5 minutes, stirring occasionally. Meanwhile, preheat a ridged chargrill pan over a high heat for 5–10 minutes.

3 Brush both sides of the polenta with oil and place in the hot pan. Cook for 2 minutes each side.

4 To serve, place 2 slices of the grilled polenta on a plate, spoon over the mushrooms and sprinkle over the Parmesan shavings.

Serves 4

50g salted butter
3 tablespoons olive oil, plus extra for brushing
1 tablespoon chopped fresh rosemary
600g mixed mushrooms, roughly sliced
2 garlic cloves, peeled and thinly sliced
50ml dry white wine
250ml double cream
20 fresh red cherry tomatoes, halved
1 x 500g block ready-cooked polenta, cut into 8 slices
50g Parmesan cheese shavings
Salt and freshly ground black pepper

ROASTED PEPPER AND TOMATO SOUP *ZUPPA DI POMODORI E PEPERONI ARROSTITI*

With its beautiful rich red colour and punchy flavours, this soup is impressive enough to be served as a first course at a dinner party. If you have time, you can roast or grill the peppers yourself, otherwise the roasted ones in jars are fine for this recipe. If you like a bit of a 'kick', try using chilli oil instead of olive oil. Serve with warm crusty bread.

1 Heat the oil in a medium saucepan over a medium heat. Add the onion and fry for 5–10 minutes, stirring occasionally.

2 Add the tomatoes and cook for about 3 minutes. Increase the heat. Stir in the stock, peppers and basil and bring to the boil. Reduce the heat. Simmer for about 10 minutes, stirring occasionally.

3 Remove the pan from the heat. Blend until smooth and season with salt and pepper.

4 Transfer the soup to warm bowls and drizzle 1 tablespoon of cream over each serving.

Serves 4

3 tablespoons extra virgin olive oil
1 medium red onion, peeled and roughly chopped
6 large ripe fresh plum tomatoes, roughly chopped
600ml hot vegetable stock
280g roasted red peppers in a jar, drained and roughly chopped
10 large fresh basil leaves
4 tablespoons double cream
Salt and freshly ground black pepper

SPINACH SOUP WITH A POACHED EGG *CREMA DI SPINACI CON UOVA IN CAMICIA*

Elegant, tasty, and delicate yet satisfying, this is a fantastic soup for a first course or light meal. It's vital to use fresh spinach for this recipe; frozen won't give you the lovely deep green colour or depth of flavour. It's also really important that the eggs are as fresh as possible for poaching. You can prepare the soup ahead, but the eggs must be poached at the last minute. Serve with warm crusty bread.

1 Heat the oil and butter in a large saucepan over a medium heat. As soon as the butter has melted, add the shallots and fry for 5 minutes. Stir in the spinach. When it has wilted, season with salt and pepper.

2 Add the cream and half the stock. Bring to the boil. As soon as it starts to boil, remove the pan from the heat. Blend using a hand-held blender until smooth (do not over blitz, or the spinach will become bitter and lose its colour). Stir in the remaining stock and taste for seasoning. Set aside.

3 Place a medium saucepan filled with 2.5 litres of hot water over a high heat. Stir in the vinegar. Bring to the boil then reduce the heat to a gentle simmer.

4 Poach the eggs in 2 batches. Break one egg into a cup. Slowly slide it into the water. Repeat for the second egg, keeping it well apart from the first so the eggs are not touching.

5 Poach very gently for 3–4 minutes or until the white is set. Keep the water at a very gentle simmer throughout to ensure the eggs do not become too hard; you just want a few bubbles breaking the surface. Using a slotted spoon, lift out the eggs and transfer to kitchen paper to drain. Repeat for the remaining eggs.

6 Ladle the soup into warmed bowls. Carefully place a poached egg in the centre. Grind over some black pepper. Serve immediately.

Serves 4

2 tablespoons extra virgin olive oil
50g salted butter
4 large shallots, peeled and finely chopped
700g fresh spinach
100ml double cream
700ml hot vegetable stock
3 tablespoons white wine vinegar
4 very fresh eggs
Salt and freshly ground black pepper

SPICY RED LENTIL SOUP *ZUPPA DI LENTICCHIE ROSSE*

Lentils are really popular in Italy, particularly the green varieties, but red lentils are also widespread in northern Italy, and make an appearance on most restaurant menus. This hearty soup, with carrots and a hint of chilli, is a real winner. If you prefer, you can use parsley instead of chives. Serve with my Cheesy ciabatta (see page 62).

1 Heat the oil in a medium saucepan over a medium heat. Add the onion and carrots and season with salt. Fry for 5–10 minutes, stirring occasionally.

2 Increase the heat. Add the stock, lentils and chilli powder and bring to the boil. Reduce the heat and simmer for 15–20 minutes or until the lentils and carrots are tender.

3 Remove the pan from the heat. Transfer 3 ladlefuls of soup into a jug and blitz until smooth using a hand-held blender. Pour the soup back into the pan and stir.

4 Ladle the soup into warm bowls and sprinkle over the chives. Serve immediately.

Serves 4

4 tablespoons extra virgin olive oil
1 red onion, peeled and finely chopped
2 large carrots, peeled and cut into
  5mm cubes
1.2 litres hot vegetable stock
100g dried red lentils, rinsed and drained
½ teaspoon chilli powder
2 tablespoons chopped fresh chives
Salt

NORTHERN ITALIAN VEGETABLE SOUP WITH CHEESY CIABATTA
MINESTRA CON CROSTINI AL FORMAGGIO

When I was filming in the Cinque Terre town of Manarola I made this soup for my guide, Giancarlo, using the wonderful fresh local ingredients. Packed full of vegetables, this soup is wholesome, hearty and flavoursome, yet light. As with most minestrone recipes, this one includes beans, but unlike many it contains no tomatoes or pasta. The cheesy ciabatta accompaniment is a great recipe to have up your sleeve, as it goes well with so many other soups and antipasti dishes.

1 Heat the oil in a large saucepan over a medium heat. Add the onion, carrots, celery, potato and cabbage and fry for about 10 minutes, stirring occasionally.

2 Pour over the stock and bring to the boil. Stir in the courgette and beans, season with salt and pepper and simmer for 20 minutes (uncovered), stirring occasionally. Stir in the tomato purée and the parsley, remove from the heat and leave to rest for 5 minutes.

3 Meanwhile, make the cheesy ciabatta. Preheat the grill to high. Put the butter in a small bowl and gradually add the pecorino. Beat together with a spoon to create a sticky paste. Set aside.

4 Toast the ciabatta on both sides. Line a baking sheet with baking parchment and place the toasts on the prepared sheet. Carefully spread over the pecorino butter and grill for 2 minutes or until the topping has melted.

5 To serve, divide the soup between warm bowls and sprinkle over the pecorino. Serve the cheesy ciabatta with the soup.

Serves 4–6

6 tablespoons extra virgin olive oil
1 large onion, peeled and chopped
2 large carrots, peeled and cut into 1cm cubes
2 celery sticks, cut into 1cm cubes
1 large baking potato, peeled and cut into 1cm cubes
100g green cabbage, roughly sliced
1.5 litres hot vegetable stock
1 courgette, cut into 1cm cubes
1 x 400g tin of cannellini beans, rinsed and drained
1 tablespoon tomato purée
2 tablespoons chopped fresh flat-leaf parsley
4 tablespoons freshly grated pecorino cheese
Salt and freshly ground black pepper

For the cheesy ciabatta
30g salted butter (room temperature)
40g freshly grated pecorino cheese
4 slices of ciabatta, cut diagonally and about 2cm thick

CCHI PASTA, PIZZA

RICE & GNOCCHI

RECIGES

SPAGHETTI WITH FRIED COURGETTES AND PEPPERS *SPAGHETTI CON ZUCCHINE E PEPERONI FRITTI*

This is a lovely light pasta dish that is particularly good in summer, when courgettes are in season. Please don't be alarmed at the amount of oil and butter required. There isn't a tomato sauce or any cream in the recipe, so you do need the oil and butter to coat the pasta. To make the dish really special, shave some truffle over the top.

1 Fill a large saucepan with 4 litres of water, add 1 tablespoon of salt and bring to the boil over a high heat.

2 Meanwhile, heat the oil and butter in a large frying pan over a medium heat. When the butter has melted, add the courgettes and peppers. Season with salt and pepper. Fry for about 25 minutes or until softened, stirring occasionally.

3 Cook the spaghetti in the boiling water (uncovered) until al dente. To get the al dente perfect bite, cook the pasta 1 minute less than instructed on the packet. Stir every minute or so.

4 Drain and tip the spaghetti back into the pan, off the heat. Add the courgette and pepper mixture and half the pecorino. Stir gently for about 20 seconds until thoroughly combined.

5 Transfer to warm plates or bowls. Sprinkle over the remaining pecorino and serve immediately.

Serves 4

10 tablespoons extra virgin olive oil
150g salted butter
2 large courgettes (about 600g), cut into
  5mm cubes
2 yellow peppers (about 400g), deseeded
  and cut into 5mm cubes
500g dried spaghetti
60g freshly grated pecorino cheese
Salt and freshly ground black pepper

FAST FUSILLI WITH GOAT'S CHEESE, CHERRY TOMATOES AND BASIL
FUSILLI VELOCI VELOCI

This is the ultimate home-cooked fast food, filling yet taking less than 20 minutes from start to finish to prepare. Make sure you buy ripe, good-quality cherry tomatoes, otherwise the dish will be flavourless. Also, use a good-quality extra virgin olive oil. If you prefer, use feta or mozzarella cheese instead of goat's cheese and Parmesan instead of pecorino. *Buon Appetito*!

1 Fill a large saucepan with 4 litres of water, add 1 tablespoon of salt and bring to the boil over a high heat.

2 Meanwhile, put the goat's cheese in a large bowl. Add the tomatoes, basil, garlic and oil. Season with salt and pepper. Stir to combine. Set aside.

3 Cook the fusilli in the boiling water (uncovered) until al dente. To get the al dente perfect bite, cook the pasta 1 minute less than instructed on the packet. Stir every minute or so.

4 Drain and tip the fusilli back into the pan. Place over a medium heat. Add the goat's cheese and tomato mixture. Stir gently for about 30 seconds to combine.

5 Transfer to warm plates or bowls. Sprinkle over the pecorino and serve immediately.

Serves 4

300g firm goat's cheese, crumbled
25 fresh red cherry tomatoes (about 350g), halved
12 fresh basil leaves
2 garlic cloves, peeled and finely sliced
6 tablespoons extra virgin olive oil
500g dried fusilli
50g freshly shaved pecorino cheese
Salt and freshly ground black pepper

ORECCHIETTE IN A SPICY TOMATO SAUCE WITH BROCCOLI *ORECHIETTE IN SALSA PICCANTE DI POMODORO CON BROCCOLI*

This dish originates in Puglia, southern Italy, but I had to include it in this book as it's one of my favourite vegetarian pasta dishes, and is incredibly quick and easy to make. The flavours are simple and delicate, with the chilli and garlic perfectly complementing the sweet Tenderstem broccoli. Orecchiette can sometimes be hard to find, but it's fine to use any shell pasta or penne rigate. For vegetarians, use rennet-free pecorino.

1 Fill a large saucepan with 4 litres of water, add 1 tablespoon of salt and bring to the boil over a high heat.

2 Meanwhile, put the oil, garlic and chilli flakes in a small saucepan and place the pan over a medium heat. Fry for 3 minutes. Add the tomatoes and season with salt. Reduce the heat and simmer for about 6 minutes, stirring occasionally.

3 Cook the orecchiette in the boiling water until al dente (about 1 minute less than stated on the packet). About 5 minutes before the end of the cooking time, drop in the broccoli (keep the water boiling).

4 Drain and tip the orecchiette and broccoli back into the pan, off the heat. Pour over the tomato mixture and stir gently for about 20 seconds to combine.

5 Transfer to warm plates or bowls. Sprinkle over the pecorino and serve immediately.

Serves 4

4 tablespoons olive oil
4 garlic cloves, peeled and finely sliced
1 teaspoon dried chilli flakes
1 x 400g tin of chopped tomatoes
500g dried orecchiette
600g Tenderstem broccoli tips, ends trimmed
50g freshly grated pecorino cheese
Salt

PENNE WITH EGGS AND PANCETTA *PENNETTE UOVA E PANCETTA*

People often ask me what my favourite pasta dish is, and this must be among my Top Ten ... salty, crisp pancetta with eggs and pecorino cheese – it's a match made in heaven. It's really important to take the saucepan off the heat when you pour over the egg mixture, otherwise you'll end up with overcooked eggs and sticky pasta. The heat from the pasta and pancetta will be enough to cook the eggs and give a creamy, moist texture.

1 Fill a large saucepan with 4 litres of water, add 1 tablespoon of salt and bring to the boil over a high heat.

2 Meanwhile, heat the oil and butter in a small frying pan over a medium heat. When the butter has melted, add the pancetta and fry for about 8 minutes, stirring occasionally. Set aside.

3 Break the eggs into a medium bowl and whisk lightly. Stir in half the pecorino and the parsley. Season with salt and pepper. Set aside.

4 Cook the penne in the boiling water (uncovered) until al dente. To get the al dente perfect bite, cook the pasta 1 minute less than instructed on the packet. Stir every minute or so.

5 Return the frying pan with the pancetta to a high heat for 1 minute.

6 Drain and tip the penne back into the pan, off the heat. Pour over the egg mixture and the pancetta with its oil. Stir for about 30 seconds to combine.

7 Transfer to warm plates or bowls. Sprinkle over the remaining pecorino and serve immediately.

Serves 4

4 tablespoons olive oil
30g salted butter
200g diced pancetta
4 medium eggs
40g freshly grated pecorino cheese
4 tablespoons chopped fresh flat-leaf
  parsley
500g dried penne rigate
Salt and freshly ground black pepper

FARFALLE WITH MUSHROOMS AND SPINACH *FARFALLE CON FUNGHI E SPINACI*

If you love creamy mushroom sauces, this vegetarian pasta dish is the one for you. When I was filming the latest TV series I prepared it at the Tuscan winery Casa al Vento for my friends Francesco and Giuseppe, after a well-deserved Chianti Classico wine bath. Yes, that's right – I bathed in red wine. Apparently, the Romans believed bathing in wine purified the skin and had rejuvenating powers. Of course, I now look 20 years younger!

1 Fill a large saucepan with 4 litres of water, add 1 tablespoon of salt and bring to the boil over a high heat.

2 Meanwhile, heat the oil, butter and thyme in a large frying pan over a high heat. Add the mushrooms, season with salt and pepper and fry for 5 minutes, stirring occasionally.

3 Add the garlic and fry for about 8 minutes. Pour over the wine and bring to the boil for 2 minutes. Reduce the heat to medium and stir in the cream and spinach. Cook for 5 minutes, stirring occasionally.

4 Cook the farfalle in the boiling water (uncovered) until al dente. To get the al dente perfect bite, cook the pasta 1 minute less than instructed on the packet. Stir every minute or so.

5 Drain and tip the farfalle into the sauce, off the heat. Add half the Parmesan. Stir for about 20 seconds to combine.

6 Transfer to warm bowls, sprinkle over the remaining Parmesan and serve immediately.

Serves 4

3 tablespoons olive oil
50g salted butter
1 tablespoon fresh thyme leaves
600g mixed wild mushrooms, cleaned and roughly sliced
2 garlic cloves, peeled and thinly sliced
100ml dry white wine
400ml double cream
2 large handfuls of fresh spinach, thick stalks removed
500g dried farfalle
30g freshly grated Parmesan cheese
Salt and freshly ground black pepper

RIGATONI WITH QUICK BOLOGNESE SAUCE *RIGATONI ALLA BOLOGNESE VELOCE*

A proper Bolognese sauce takes hours to cook, but we don't all have the time. This is a quick but delicious way to make it in under 30 minutes, from start to finish. If you prefer, you can use pork instead of beef, or a combination of the two. Lamb also works well. If you have any sauce left over, serve it the following day on a jacket potato. Alternatively, you can freeze it.

1 Fill a large saucepan with 4 litres of water, add 1 tablespoon of salt and bring to the boil over a high heat.

2 Meanwhile, put the oil and garlic in a medium saucepan and place over a medium heat. As soon as the garlic starts to sizzle, add the mince and fry for about 8 minutes or until well browned, stirring with a wooden spoon to break up the meat.

3 Increase the heat, pour over the wine and let it bubble for 2 minutes. Add the tomatoes, and basil, and season with salt and pepper. Reduce the heat and simmer for 20 minutes, stirring occasionally.

4 Cook the rigatoni in the boiling water (uncovered) until al dente. To get the al dente perfect bite, cook the pasta 1 minute less than instructed on the packet. Stir every minute or so.

5 Drain and tip the rigatoni back into the pan, off the heat. Pour over the sauce and add half the Parmesan. Stir for about 20 seconds to combine.

6 Transfer to warm plates or bowls. Sprinkle over the remaining Parmesan and serve immediately.

Serves 4

4 tablespoons olive oil
4 garlic cloves, peeled and thinly sliced
500g minced beef
100ml red wine
2 x 400g tins of chopped tomatoes
10 fresh basil leaves
500g dried rigatoni
60g freshly grated Parmesan cheese
Salt and freshly ground black pepper

PASTA SHELLS WITH PEAS, PANCETTA AND EGGS *CONCHIGLIE CON PISELLI, PANCETTA E UOVA*

This pasta dish starts in a similar way to a soup and slowly develops into the most delicious pasta dish. In Italy we often combine peas and pancetta – the combination of sweet and salty works beautifully. Fresh peas are best, but frozen peas are absolutely fine for this recipe. *Pasta piselli* is often made without meat, but I do think the pancetta takes it to a different level.

1 Heat the oil in a large saucepan over a high heat. Add the onion and pancetta and fry for 15 minutes, stirring occasionally. Add the peas and fry for 5 minutes.

2 Pour over the stock, bring to the boil then reduce the heat to medium. Season with salt and pepper. Simmer for 25 minutes, stirring occasionally.

3 Add the pasta shells and cook for about 12 minutes, stirring frequently.

4 Remove the pan from the heat. Add the eggs and Parmesan. Stir gently for about 20 seconds to combine and create a creamy texture. Serve immediately.

Serves 4

6 tablespoons olive oil
1 large onion, peeled and chopped
150g diced pancetta
500g frozen peas, defrosted
2 litres hot vegetable stock
500g dried medium pasta shells
3 medium eggs, beaten
50g freshly grated Parmesan cheese
Salt and freshly ground black pepper

LINGUINE WITH A SPICY PANCETTA, CHERRY TOMATO AND BASIL SAUCE
LINGUINE ALLA LUCIANO

This is my son Luciano's favourite pasta dish. He loves the spicy pancetta with the sweet basil sauce. If you want to make it for vegetarians, replace the pancetta with 1 large courgette chopped into 5mm cubes and replace the pecorino with rennet-free cheese.

1 Fill a large saucepan with 4 litres of water, add 1 tablespoon of salt and bring to the boil over a high heat.

2 Meanwhile, heat the olive oil in a small frying pan over a medium heat. Add the chilli flakes and pancetta and fry for 20 minutes, stirring occasionally. Set aside.

3 Pour the extra virgin olive oil into a food processor and add the garlic. Blitz for about 1 minute. Add the basil and blitz for 1 further minute or until smooth. Set aside.

4 Cook the linguine in the boiling water (uncovered) until al dente. To get the al dente perfect bite, cook the pasta 1 minute less than instructed on the packet. Stir every minute or so.

5 Drain and tip the linguine back into the pan, off the heat. Add the pancetta and chilli, the basil sauce and the tomatoes. Stir gently for about 20 seconds to combine.

6 Transfer the pasta to warm plates or bowls. Sprinkle over the pecorino and serve immediately.

Serves 4

3 tablespoons olive oil
2 teaspoons dried chilli flakes
200g diced pancetta
150ml extra virgin olive oil
2 large garlic cloves, peeled and halved
50g fresh basil leaves
500g dried linguine
20 fresh red cherry tomatoes, halved
50g freshly grated pecorino cheese
Salt

FETTUCCINE WITH MINCED PORK, MASCARPONE AND WHITE TRUFFLE OIL *FETTUCCINE CON MAIALE, MASCARPONE E OLIO DI TARTUFO BIANCO*

When I visited Turin for the latest TV series I was lucky enough to drive a vintage Fiat 500 around the Lingotto racetrack on top of the old Fiat factory, fulfilling a childhood dream. I then had the pleasure of cooking this delicious pasta dish right in the middle of the track for my city guides and new friends, Carlo, Massimo and Laura. It is a day that I will never forget.

1 Fill a large saucepan with 4 litres of water, add 1 tablespoon of salt and bring to the boil over a high heat.

2 Meanwhile, heat the oil, butter and rosemary in a medium saucepan over a medium heat. As soon as the rosemary starts to sizzle, add the onion and fry for about 8 minutes, stirring occasionally.

3 Add the pork, season with salt and pepper and fry for 15 minutes, stirring frequently. Stir in the mascarpone, peas and parsley and cook for 1 minute.

4 Cook the fettuccine in the boiling water (uncovered) until al dente. To get the al dente perfect bite, cook the pasta 1 minute less than instructed on the packet. Stir every minute or so. Scoop out a cupful of the cooking water and stir about 2 tablespoons into the sauce.

5 Remove the fettuccine from the water using tongs or a spaghetti spoon and put it directly in the pan with the sauce without draining. Toss for about 20 seconds to coat the pasta. Stir in the pecorino.

6 To serve, divide among warm plates and drizzle over the truffle oil.

Serves 4

4 tablespoons olive oil
100g salted butter
1 tablespoon chopped fresh rosemary
1 large onion, peeled and finely chopped
500g minced pork
250g mascarpone cheese
150g frozen peas, defrosted
2 tablespoons chopped fresh flat-leaf parsley
350g dried fettuccine
60g freshly grated pecorino cheese
4 tablespoons white truffle olive oil
Salt and freshly ground black pepper

GORGONZOLA AND PARMA HAM PIZZA *PIZZA GORGONZOLA E PROSCIUTTO CRUDO*

Gorgonzola and Parma ham both originate in northern Italy and make a great combination. I often prepare this pizza for my boys, and sometimes we ring the changes by using cooked ham or salami instead of Parma ham. Make sure you preheat the oven to the correct temperature before putting in the pizza, or the dough will be soggy and not cook properly.

1 To make the dough, put the flour, yeast and salt in a large bowl. Make a well in the centre and add the oil then gradually pour in 140ml of warm water.

2 Using the handle of a wooden spoon, mix together thoroughly to create a wet dough. Turn out the dough onto a well-floured surface and knead for about 5 minutes or until smooth and elastic.

3 Brush 2 large baking sheets with oil. Halve the dough and shape into 2 equal-sized balls. Place each in the centre of the oiled baking sheets. Brush the top of the dough with a little oil and cover with cling film. Leave to rest at room temperature for 15 minutes. Preheat the oven to 220°C/gas mark 7.

4 Meanwhile, make the topping. In a measuring jug or medium bowl, combine the passata and 2 tablespoons of the oil. Season with salt and pepper. Set aside.

5 Use your hands to push each dough ball out from the centre, stretching the dough to create 2 rounds about 25cm in diameter and 1–2cm thick. You can also use a rolling pin if you prefer. Make a small rim by pulling up the edges slightly.

6 Using the back of a tablespoon, spread the tomato mixture evenly over the pizza bases, from the centre outwards, avoiding the rim. Scatter over the mozzarella and Gorgonzola.

7 Bake for 12–15 minutes or until golden brown. Remove from the oven, arrange the ham on top and return to the oven for 1 further minute to heat through.

Makes 2

200g strong white flour, plus extra for dusting
1 x 7g sachet of fast-action (easy-blend) dried yeast
½ teaspoon salt
2 tablespoons extra virgin olive oil, plus extra for greasing and brushing

For the topping
150ml passata (sieved tomatoes)
4 tablespoons extra virgin olive oil
1 x 125g ball of mozzarella cheese, drained and cut into small cubes
100g Gorgonzola cheese
6 slices Parma ham
Salt and freshly ground black pepper

FONTINA, MOZZARELLA, GARLIC AND ROSEMARY PIZZA *PIZZA AGLIO, FONTINA, MOZZARELLA E ROSMARINO*

A rectangular pizza cut into squares is ideal for sharing and makes fantastic party food. It's also great for days when you don't feel like having a whole pizza to yourself. I love this cheese and garlic topping. Fontina, which is produced in northern Italy's Val d'Aosta, has a lovely buttery, nutty flavour. If you can't find it, you can use Taleggio or Gorgonzola (which has a stronger taste) instead.

1 First make the dough (see steps 1–2, page 88).

2 Brush a traybake tin, about 30 x 40cm, with oil. Shape the dough into a ball and place in the centre of the oiled tin. Brush the top of the dough with a little oil and cover with cling film. Leave to rest at room temperature for 20 minutes. Preheat the oven to 220°C/ gas mark 7.

3 Use your hands to push the dough ball out from the centre, stretching the dough to reach the edges of the tin.

4 Scatter the fontina, mozzarella, garlic and rosemary over the pizza. Grind over some black pepper. Bake for about 15 minutes or until golden brown.

Serves 2

200g strong white flour, plus extra for dusting
1 x 7g sachet of fast-action (easy-blend) dried yeast
½ teaspoon salt
2 tablespoons extra virgin olive oil, plus extra for greasing and brushing

For the topping
150g fontina cheese, rind removed and cut into small cubes
1 x 125g ball of mozzarella cheese, drained and cut into small cubes
3 garlic cloves, peeled and finely chopped
2 tablespoons fresh rosemary leaves
Freshly ground black pepper

PIZZA WITH SPICY SALAMI *PIZZA CON SALAME PICCANTE*

This is the pizza I like to cook for my friends when they come to my house for a 'boys' night'. It's the perfect accompaniment to a few beers. In Italy spicy salami is called *salame piccante* or *salamino piccante*, and you won't find anything called a pepperoni pizza (pepperoni is the Italian-American version of *salame piccante*). However, confusingly, you might find a peperoni pizza (pronounced the same but with one less 'p'), which would be topped with bell peppers. If you like, you can use chorizo for this recipe.

1 First make the dough (see steps 1–3, page 88).

2 Meanwhile, make the topping. In a measuring jug or medium bowl, combine the passata and the oil. Season with salt. Set aside.

3 Use your hands to push each dough ball out from the centre, stretching the dough to create 2 rounds about 25cm in diameter and 1–2cm thick. You can also use a rolling pin if you prefer. Make a small rim by pulling up the edges slightly.

4 Using the back of a tablespoon, spread the tomato mixture evenly over the pizza bases, from the centre outwards, avoiding the rim. Scatter over the mozzarella.

5 Bake for 8 minutes. Remove from the oven, scatter over the salami and bake for a further 5–8 minutes or until golden brown.

Makes 2

200g strong white flour, plus extra for dusting
1 x 7g sachet of fast-action (easy-blend) dried yeast
½ teaspoon salt
2 tablespoons extra virgin olive oil, plus extra for greasing and brushing

For the topping
150ml passata (sieved tomatoes)
2 tablespoons extra virgin olive oil
2 x 150g balls of mozzarella cheese, drained and cut into small cubes
12 slices of spicy salami
Salt

SHORT-CUT PIZZA MARGHERITA *PIZZA MARGHERITA VELOCISSIMA*

OK, I admit this isn't the traditional Neapolitan way to make a Margherita pizza, but trust me, if you're short on time and you want a quick, tasty pizza, this is a really great choice. Once you've made the dough (which you can do ahead), it will take you under 30 minutes to prepare and cook. It will taste so much better than one of those poor-quality, deep-pan pizzas you can buy or order, as well as so much less expensive, and you'll feel great because you made it yourself.

1 First make the dough (see steps 1–3, page 88).

2 Meanwhile, make the topping. In a measuring jug or medium bowl, combine the passata and the oil. Season with salt and pepper. Set aside.

3 Use your hands to push each dough ball out from the centre, stretching the dough to create 2 rounds about 25cm in diameter and 1–2cm thick. You can also use a rolling pin if you prefer. Make a small rim by pulling up the edges slightly.

4 Using the back of a tablespoon, spread the tomato mixture evenly over the pizza bases, from the centre outwards, avoiding the rim. Scatter over the mozzarella.

5 Bake for 12–15 minutes or until golden brown. Remove from the oven, scatter over the basil and return to the oven for 1 further minute.

Makes 2

200g strong white flour, plus extra for dusting
1 x 7g sachet of fast-action (easy-blend) dried yeast
½ teaspoon salt
2 tablespoons extra virgin olive oil, plus extra for greasing and brushing

For the topping
150ml passata (sieved tomatoes)
2 tablespoons extra virgin olive oil
2 x 150g balls of mozzarella cheese, drained and cut into small cubes
8–10 fresh basil leaves
Salt and freshly ground black pepper

TOMATO, CHILLI, GARLIC AND OREGANO PIZZA *PIZZA ARRABBIATA*

The Italian word *arrabbiata* means 'angry', and refers to the 'angry' heat of chillies. So if you like it hot, this is the pizza for you. Please don't be tempted to add any cheese – *pizza arrabbiata* should always be unadulterated heat. However, a few anchovies on top works very well.

1 First make the dough (see steps 1–3, page 88).

2 Meanwhile, make the topping. In a measuring jug or medium bowl, combine the tomatoes, 2 tablespoons of the oil, the garlic, chilli flakes and oregano, Season with salt. Using your fingertips, squeeze the tomatoes to create a fine pulp. Set aside.

3 Use your hands to push each dough ball out from the centre, stretching the dough to create 2 rounds about 25cm in diameter and 1–2cm thick. You can also use a rolling pin if you prefer. Make a small rim by pulling up the edges slightly.

4 Using the back of a tablespoon, spread the tomato mixture evenly over the pizza bases, from the centre outwards, avoiding the rim.

5 Bake for 12–15 minutes or until golden brown. Remove from the oven, drizzle 1 tablespoon of oil over each pizza and return to the oven for 1 further minute.

Makes 2

200g strong white flour, plus extra for
  dusting
1 x 7g sachet of fast-action (easy-blend)
  dried yeast
½ teaspoon salt
2 tablespoons extra virgin olive oil, plus
  extra for greasing and brushing

For the topping
200g tinned chopped tomatoes
4 tablespoons extra virgin olive oil
3 garlic cloves, peeled and finely chopped
1 teaspoon dried chilli flakes
1 teaspoon dried oregano
Salt

WHITE PIZZA WITH MOZZARELLA, MASCARPONE AND PECORINO
PIZZA BIANCA

Pizza bianca (white pizza) is a must-try, especially for those who don't like tomato sauce. It's particularly popular in Rome, where the pizza base is sometimes simply sprinkled with salt. I like to make mine with cheese, as it gives a wonderful flavour and texture. If you like, you can use ricotta cheese instead of mascarpone and can add a few slices of Parma ham.

1 First make the dough (see steps 1–3, page 88).

2 Use your hands to push each dough ball out from the centre, stretching the dough to create 2 rounds about 25cm in diameter and 1–2cm thick. You can also use a rolling pin if you prefer. Make a small rim by pulling up the edges slightly.

3 Make the topping. Scatter over the mozzarella. Using a teaspoon, dot the pizza with mascarpone. Grind over some black pepper.

4 Bake for 12–14 minutes or until golden brown. Remove from the oven, sprinkle over the pecorino and return to the oven for a further 2 minutes.

Makes 2

200g strong white flour, plus extra for dusting
1 x 7g sachet of fast-action (easy-blend) dried yeast
½ teaspoon salt
2 tablespoons extra virgin olive oil, plus extra for greasing and brushing

For the topping
1 x 150g ball of mozzarella cheese, drained and cut into small cubes
100g mascarpone cheese
20g freshly grated pecorino cheese
Freshly ground black pepper

ASPARAGUS, PEA AND PRAWN RISOTTO *RISOTTO ASPARAGI, PISELLI E GAMBERONI*

This is the best-selling risotto in my restaurants, and is a really lovely, fresh-tasting recipe for spring, when asparagus is in season. Make sure you don't overcook the prawns, as they can easily become tough. For a special occasion you might like to use scallops instead of prawns.

1 Heat the oil in a heavy-based saucepan or large, high-sided frying pan over a medium heat. Add the leeks and fry for 5–10 minutes or until softened, stirring frequently.

2 Add the rice and fry for about 3 minutes, stirring continuously, until the grains are coated and shiny. Pour over the wine and let it bubble for 1–2 minutes or until evaporated.

3 Add 2 ladlesful of stock and bring to a simmer. Stir continuously until the liquid has been absorbed. Stir in the asparagus and peas.

4 Continue adding the rest of the stock in the same way, until the rice is cooked but still has a slight bite. This will take about 18 minutes. You may not need to add all the stock.

5 Remove the pan from the heat. Add the butter cubes and the pecorino and stir for about 30 seconds until creamy. Season with salt and pepper. Keep warm.

6 Heat the remaining butter in a medium frying pan over a high heat. As soon as the butter starts to sizzle, add the prawns and fry for about 1 minute each side. Season with salt and pepper.

7 To serve, spoon the risotto onto warm plates and place the prawns on top.

Serves 6

8 tablespoons olive oil
2 medium leeks, halved lengthways
  and finely sliced
500g Arborio or Carnaroli rice
200ml dry white wine
1.5 litres hot vegetable stock
250g fine asparagus spears, woody
  ends removed and sliced diagonally
  into 2cm lengths
250g frozen peas, defrosted
60g salted butter, cut into cubes, plus
  40g for frying
60g freshly grated pecorino cheese
12 raw, peeled large king prawns, deveined
Salt and freshly ground black pepper

MAMMA'S CHICKEN RISOTTO *RISOTTO AL POMODORO E POLLO*

My mother used to cook this risotto for my sister and me every week, as it's so tasty and easy and we loved it. There are several variations – without chicken, which still tastes good, and with pork loin instead of chicken, which makes a delicious change. Serve with a good bottle of full-bodied Italian red wine.

1 Heat the oil in a heavy-based saucepan or large, high-sided frying pan over a medium heat. Add the onions and fry for 5–10 minutes or until softened but not browned, stirring frequently. Add the chicken and fry for about 5 minutes or until golden brown, stirring occasionally.

2 Add the rice and fry for about 3 minutes, stirring continuously, until the grains are coated and shiny. Pour over the wine and let it bubble for 1–2 minutes or until evaporated.

3 Add 2 ladlesful of stock and the passata. Bring to a simmer. Stir continuously until the liquid has been absorbed. Continue adding the rest of the stock in the same way, until the rice is cooked but still has a slight bite. This will take about 18 minutes. You may not need to add all the stock.

4 Remove the pan from the heat. Add the butter, pecorino and parsley. Stir for about 30 seconds until creamy. Season with salt and pepper. Top with a little extra parsley and pecorino.

5 To serve, spoon the risotto onto warm plates. Drizzle 1 tablespoon of oil over each serving.

Serves 6

8 tablespoons olive oil

2 medium red onions, peeled and finely chopped

2 skinless, boneless chicken breasts (about 400g in total), cut into 1cm chunks

500g Arborio or Carnaroli rice

200ml dry white wine

1 litre hot vegetable stock

400ml passata (sieved tomatoes)

60g salted butter, cut into cubes

60g freshly grated pecorino cheese, plus extra to garnish

3 tablespoons chopped fresh flat-leaf parsley, plus extra to serve

4 tablespoons extra virgin olive oil

Salt and freshly ground black pepper

MILANESE-STYLE RISOTTO *RISOTTO ALLA MILANESE*

As I was filming *Gino's Italian Express* in northern Italy, I stayed in over 25 different hotels, including Milan, Turin, Verona, Bologna, Pisa and Bergamo. Every hotel I stayed in served *Risotto alla Milanese* and I ordered this dish at least 15 times. I just love its simplicity, vibrant colour and saffron flavour. This risotto is perfect on its own, but it can also be served as an accompaniment to a main course. If you can't find saffron threads, saffron powder will do the job.

1 Heat the oil and half the butter in a large, heavy-based saucepan over a medium heat. Add the onion and fry for about 8 minutes or until softened but not browned, stirring occasionally.

2 Add the rice and fry for about 3 minutes, stirring continuously. Stir in the saffron. Pour in the wine and simmer for about 1 minute or until reduced by half.

3 Add a couple of ladlesful of stock and bring to a simmer. Reduce the heat and stir continuously until all the liquid has been absorbed.

4 Continue adding the rest of the stock in the same way, until the rice is cooked but still has a slight bite. It will take about 16–18 minutes and you may not need to add all the stock.

5 Remove the pan from the heat. Add the remaining butter and the Parmesan. Season with salt and pepper. Stir vigorously for 20 seconds until well combined and creamy in texture.

Serves 6

4 tablespoons olive oil
150g salted butter, cut into cubes
1 large onion, peeled and finely chopped
500g Arborio or Carnaroli rice
Large pinch of saffron threads (about ¾ teaspoon)
200ml dry white wine
1.5 litres hot chicken stock
100g freshly grated Parmesan cheese
Salt and freshly ground black pepper

GNOCCHI WITH A TOMATO, MOZZARELLA AND BASIL SAUCE *GNOCCHI MARGHERITA*

Gnocchi (small dumplings) are an Italian staple, particularly in northern Italy. They're usually made with potato, but homemade gnocchi are made from all sorts of ingredients, including spinach, ricotta and pumpkin. When you buy gnocchi from a deli or supermarket, choose a brand that contains at least 70 per cent potatoes, or they will be tasteless and have a stodgy texture. This recipe is really quick and easy, and is often a hit with kids.

1 Heat the oil in a medium saucepan over a medium heat. Add the onion and fry for 10 minutes, stirring occasionally.

2 Add the tomatoes and basil and season with salt and pepper. Reduce the heat and simmer gently for 10 minutes, stirring occasionally. Meanwhile, bring a large saucepan of salted water to the boil.

3 Drop the gnocchi into the boiling water and cook for 2–3 minutes or until they float to the surface. Drain and tip them back into the pan, off the heat.

4 Pour over the tomato sauce and add the mozzarella. Stir gently for about 10–20 seconds or until the mozzarella has melted slightly.

5 Transfer the gnocchi to warm plates. Sprinkle over the pecorino and serve immediately.

Serves 4

4 tablespoons extra virgin olive oil
1 large red onion, peeled and finely sliced
2 x 400g tins of chopped tomatoes
5 large fresh basil leaves
500g shop-bought potato gnocchi
  (minimum 70% potato)
2 x 125g balls of mozzarella cheese,
  drained and cut into small cubes
40g freshly grated pecorino cheese
Salt and freshly ground black pepper

ES MAIN COURSES

RECITES

COD WITH POTATOES, CHERRY TOMATOES, CAPERS AND OLIVES
MERLUZZO IN ACQUA PAZZA

The northern Italians use cod quite a lot, and it's usually cooked very simply, as in this classic recipe (*Acqua pazza* means 'crazy water'). Containing potatoes, it's a great one-pot supper dish. The same recipe works well with any firm white, flaky fish and salmon. Make sure you don't overcook the fish, as it can become dry, and resist the urge to turn it too much or too early, as it will flake apart.

1 Cook the potatoes in boiling salted water for about 15 minutes or until they feel tender when pierced with a knife. Drain and set aside to cool. Cut in half.

2 Heat the butter, oil, capers, olives and thyme in a large frying pan over a high heat. As soon as the butter starts to sizzle, lay the cod in the pan, skin-side down, and fry gently for 2–4 minutes (depending on the thickness) or until golden. Carefully turn and fry for a further 2–4 minutes.

3 Using a slotted spoon, lift the fillets and transfer to a warm dish. Season with salt and pepper. Cover with foil and set aside.

4 Pour the wine into the frying pan and let it bubble for 1 minute. Stir to scrape up the sticky bits on the bottom of the pan. Add the boiled potatoes and tomatoes, and season with salt and pepper. Stir thoroughly and cook for about 2 minutes.

5 To serve, spoon the potato mixture in the centre of each plate and gently place the cod fillets on top, skin-side down. Drizzle over any pan juices. Serve immediately.

Serves 4

500g baby potatoes, scrubbed
50g salted butter
3 tablespoons olive oil
2 tablespoons capers, drained
150g pitted green olives, drained
1 tablespoon fresh thyme leaves
4 x 150g cod fillets (skin on)
150ml dry white wine
300g fresh red cherry tomatoes
Salt and freshly ground black pepper

ITALIAN SWEET AND SOUR GRILLED SALMON *SALMONE MARINATO AL MIELE E ACETO BALSAMICO*

Salmon is a healthy, oily fish that works really well with sweet-sour (*agrodolce*) flavours – a combination that is popular in Italy, particularly in Sicily. Here I've given instructions for grilling, but it's also a great recipe to try on the barbecue. If you like, you can use soy sauce instead of balsamic vinegar; just remember not to add any salt to the marinade. Serve with boiled new potatoes dressed with a little extra virgin olive oil, balsamic vinegar, and salt and pepper.

1 First make the marinade. Put the vinegar and honey in a non-metallic medium bowl. Whisk to combine. Gradually add the oil, whisking vigorously as you go. Stir in the parsley and garlic, and season with salt and pepper. Set aside.

2 Gently place the salmon fillets in the marinade. Cover with cling film and leave to marinate for 15 minutes at room temperature. Halfway through the marinating period, carefully move the salmon around to ensure it is all coated.

3 Preheat the grill to its highest setting. Line a baking sheet with foil. Using a fish slice, carefully remove the salmon fillets from the marinade and place on the prepared baking sheet. Discard the marinade.

4 Grill the salmon for 6–8 minutes. To test if the salmon is done, pull back a small piece of flesh with a fork. It should flake easily and no longer look opaque inside. Make sure you do not overcook the fish, or it will become dry. Serve immediately.

Serves 4

4 tablespoons balsamic vinegar
3 tablespoons runny honey
3 tablespoons extra virgin olive oil
3 tablespoons chopped fresh flat-leaf parsley
1 garlic clove, peeled and crushed
4 x 150g salmon fillets (skin removed)
Salt and freshly ground black pepper

TUNA STEAKS IN A GARLIC, LEMON, CHIVE AND CHILLI CRUST

TONNO IN CROSTA D'AGLIO, LIMONE, ERBA CIPOLLINA E PEPERONCINO

When I was filming in Pisa I saw this dish in many restaurants, so out of curiosity I had to try it. It was really delicious and fresh-tasting, and I loved the contrast of textures between the crisp crust and the tuna steak. The people of Pisa are, quite rightly, very proud of this dish, so I decided to share the recipe with you all. Serve with a crispy salad and enjoy!

1 Preheat the grill to its highest setting. Brush a baking sheet with oil and set aside.

2 Put all the ingredients for the crust in a food processor and blitz to fine crumbs. If the mixture seems too wet, add one more slice of bread. Transfer to a large plate or tray.

3 Dip the tuna steaks into the breadcrumb mixture until evenly coated. Press the breadcrumbs into the tuna so that they stick. Transfer the steaks to the prepared baking sheet.

4 Grill the tuna for 3 minutes each side or until golden (make sure the tray is not too close to the heat, otherwise the breadcrumbs will burn). Serve immediately with lemon wedges.

Serves 4

4 tuna steaks (about 200g each)
Lemon wedges to serve

For the crust
8 slices bread (white or brown, preferably 1 day old), crusts removed and torn
3 garlic cloves, peeled and crushed
3 tablespoons chopped fresh chives
1 teaspoon dried chilli flakes
Juice of 1 lemon
1 tablespoon extra virgin olive oil, plus extra for brushing
Salt

WHOLE ROASTED SEA BASS WITH ROSEMARY, LEMON AND POTATOES
SPIGOLA AL FORNO CON ROSMARINO, LIMONE E PATATE

I love serving a large, whole roasted fish with potatoes like this at the table – it's so theatrical somehow. It also tastes superb – the fish is succulent and moist, and the potatoes are crisp with a wonderful flavour, having absorbed the juices from the fish. It's a real favourite with my children, Luciano, Rocco and Mia. The only drawback is portioning the fish, but once you've tried it a few times it will become easier, I promise!

1 Preheat the oven to 180°C/gas mark 4. Rinse the fish under cold running water and pat dry with kitchen paper.

2 Grease a large roasting tin (about 35 x 40cm) with oil. Place the sea bass diagonally in the tin and brush with 2 tablespoons of the oil. Stuff the stomach cavity with the lemon, rosemary and garlic. Set aside.

3 Put the potatoes in a large bowl and drizzle over the remaining 3 tablespoons of oil. Sprinkle over the oregano, and season with salt and pepper. Mix with your hands to ensure the potatoes are completely coated in the seasoned oil.

4 Arrange the potatoes around the fish. Roast for 40 minutes.

5 Meanwhile, prepare the dressing. Put the lemon juice, 2 tablespoons of cold water and some salt in a small bowl. Gradually add the oil and whisk thoroughly until well combined. Set aside.

6 To portion the fish, remove and discard the lemon, rosemary and garlic and carefully transfer the fish to a board. Cut off and discard the tail. Using a thin-bladed knife and starting just behind the head, carefully cut along the backbone towards the tail end. Gently pull away the skin.

7 Using a palette knife, carefully lift the top fillet and place it skinned-side down alongside the fish. Scrape away any tiny bones and remove any dark flesh. Carefully lift the spine from the bottom fillet and discard. Remove any stray bones and dark flesh from the bottom fillet. Cut off and discard the head. Slice each fillet in half.

8 To serve, divide the potatoes among 4 warm plates and place a fish portion alongside. Drizzle over the dressing and serve immediately.

Serves 4

1 whole sea bass (about 1.3kg), gutted and scaled
5 tablespoons extra virgin olive oil, plus extra for greasing
2 slices of lemon, about 1cm thick
2 rosemary sprigs
2 garlic cloves, peeled
600g medium potatoes (e.g. Maris Piper), peeled and very thinly sliced
1 teaspoon dried oregano
Juice of 1 whole lemon
5 tablespoons extra virgin olive oil
Salt and freshly ground black pepper

CHICKEN AND PANCETTA COOKED IN BEER *POLLO COTTO IN BIRRA E PANCETTA*

Whenever I cook this chicken recipe it always reminds me of Cecilia, a wonderful lady I met in Florence. She is a member of *Le Cesarine*, the network of home cooks who open their doors to the public. Guests pay to have an authentic dining experience in a local's home, and the host shares their recipes with the aim of keeping traditional Italian cooking alive. I took part in one of these evenings and cooked this dish for her guests. Serve with my Roasted new potatoes (see page 174).

1 Put the onion and rosemary in a large shallow casserole or sauté pan. Add the oil, season the onions with salt and add the pancetta. Fry over a high heat for about 8 minutes or until softened and lightly golden, stirring occasionally.

2 Add the chicken, skin-side down, and fry for about 8 minutes or until golden brown. Turn and fry for a further 2 minutes.

3 Pour the beer over the chicken, add the bouillon powder and bring to the boil. Reduce the heat to medium and simmer for 10 minutes (uncovered), stirring occasionally.

4 Turn the chicken and cook for a further 10 minutes. Turn the chicken once more, season with pepper and cook for a further 15 minutes or until cooked through.

5 To serve, place 2 chicken thighs on each warm plate and spoon over the sauce.

Serves 4

1 large onion, peeled and chopped
1 tablespoon chopped fresh rosemary
4 tablespoons olive oil
150g pancetta, chopped
8 bone-in, skin-on chicken thighs (about 1kg in total)
2 bottles of lager (about 660ml in total)
½ teaspoon vegetable bouillon powder
Salt and freshly ground black pepper

CHICKEN BREASTS IN A LEMON AND CAPER SAUCE *PETTI DI POLLO AL LIMONE E CAPPERI*

Although the combination of lemon and capers is commonly used in fish dishes, it works just as well with chicken. The sharpness of the lemon and the salty tanginess of the capers contrast beautifully with the delicate flavour of the meat. You can also use veal for this recipe. Serve with potatoes or rice, and a green vegetable or side salad.

1 Cut each chicken breast horizontally in half to produce 2 thin slices. Put the flour on a large plate and season with salt and pepper. Dip the chicken in the seasoned flour to lightly coat. Shake off any excess flour.

2 Heat the oil and half the butter in a large frying pan over a medium heat. Once the butter has melted, add the chicken and fry for 5–6 minutes each side or until golden brown and cooked through. Using a slotted spoon, transfer the chicken to a warmed dish and cover with foil to keep warm.

3 Make the sauce. Add the lemon juice, stock and capers to the pan juices. Stir and scrape the bottom of the pan to release any sticky bits left from the chicken. Bring to the boil, stirring, and boil for 1 minute. Add the parsley and remaining butter and simmer for 1 further minute, stirring until blended.

4 To serve, place 2 slices of chicken on a warm plate and drizzle over the sauce. Serve immediately.

Serves 4

4 skinless, boneless chicken breasts (about 800g in total)
60g plain flour
4 tablespoons olive oil
80g salted butter
Juice of 2 lemons
50ml hot chicken stock
2 tablespoons nonpareille capers, drained
4 tablespoons chopped fresh flat-leaf parsley
Salt and freshly ground black pepper

ROASTED CHICKEN THIGHS IN A HONEY, CHILLI AND BALSAMIC GLAZE
POLLO ARROSTO CON MIELE, PEPERONCINO E GLASSA DI ACETO BALSAMICO

I love chicken thighs, and this is one of my favourite recipes – it's so simple and appetising. I've tried the same recipe with chicken breasts, but it didn't work as well – the thigh meat stays succulent, whereas the breasts dry out. Don't cover the dish when roasting the chicken, or you'll create steam and won't get such a lovely crisp, caramelised skin. Serve with a simple green salad dressed with extra virgin olive oil, freshly squeezed lemon juice and a little salt.

1 First make the marinade. Combine the honey and balsamic glaze in a small bowl. Gradually add the oil, whisking as you go. Place the chicken in a non-metallic baking dish and drizzle over the marinade. Sprinkle over the rosemary, chilli flakes and some salt.

2 Use your hands to massage the marinade and seasonings into the chicken. Place the chicken skin-side down. Leave to marinate for 15 minutes at room temperature. Meanwhile, preheat the oven to 200°C/gas mark 6.

3 Roast the chicken for 15 minutes, then turn and roast for a further 35 minutes or until golden brown and cooked through.

Serves 4

2 tablespoons runny honey
2 tablespoons balsamic glaze
3 tablespoons olive oil
2 tablespoons chopped fresh rosemary
1 teaspoon dried chilli flakes
8 bone-in chicken thighs (about 1kg
 in total, skin on), trimmed
Salt

CHICKEN BREASTS IN A SWEET VERMOUTH SAUCE *POLLO AL MARTINI BIANCO*

Italians love a glass of sweet vermouth, usually Martini Bianco. My favourite way to drink it is to add a few cubes of ice, a cheeky shot of vodka and a lemon twist, but I also like to cook with it. This is a really easy recipe that will leave you wanting more. It's important to use sweet vermouth, not dry. If you prefer, you can use a sweet sherry or an Italian dessert wine, such as vin santo, instead.

1 Cut each chicken breast horizontally in half to produce 2 thin slices. Put the flour on a large plate and season with salt and pepper. Dip the chicken in the seasoned flour to lightly coat. Shake off any excess flour.

2 Heat the oil and half the butter in a large frying pan over a medium heat. Once the butter has melted, add the chicken and fry for 5–6 minutes or until golden brown. Turn the chicken and cook for a further 2 minutes.

3 Pour in the vermouth and let it bubble for about 2 minutes or until it has evaporated, shaking the pan occasionally.

4 Add the remaining butter and sprinkle over some salt. Cook for a further 2 minutes, stirring continuously until blended.

5 To serve, place 2 slices of chicken on a warm plate and drizzle over the sauce. Serve immediately.

Serves 4

4 skinless, boneless chicken breasts (about 800g in total)
60g plain flour
4 tablespoons olive oil
80g salted butter
150ml sweet vermouth (e.g. Martini Bianco)
Salt and freshly ground black pepper

HAMBURGERS WITH SPICY MAYONNAISE AND EMMENTAL *HAMBURGER CON MAIONESE PICCANTE ED EMMENTAL*

This may seem like an unusual choice in an Italian cookery book, but I was given this recipe by a lady called Veronica, whom I met when filming in her house in Veneto. She very kindly made these burgers for me and all the crew, and they were a huge success. The balsamic glaze gives them a bit of an Italian twist. I've added the spicy mayonnaise because I think it works really well with the Emmental cheese. Serve with a bottle of cold Italian beer.

1 Place the mince in a large bowl with the caramelised onion chutney and balsamic glaze, and season with salt and pepper. Mix with your hands until thoroughly combined.

2 Using dampened hands, divide the mixture into 4 equal-sized balls. Place on a board and press the balls down gently with your hands to flatten into patties about 10cm across. Set aside.

3 Preheat a ridged cast-iron chargrill pan over a high heat for 5–10 minutes. Meanwhile, put the mayonnaise in a small bowl. Stir in the Tabasco. Set aside.

4 Brush both sides of the patties with a little oil and place them in the hot pan. Cook for 2–3 minutes each side for medium rare burgers, pressing down with a fish slice. If you prefer your burgers medium to well done, cook for a further 1–2 minutes each side. Transfer to a warm dish for 1 minute or so and cover with foil.

5 Meanwhile, toast your burger buns. Spread all the buns with the spicy mayonnaise. Place the burgers on the bottom buns, cover with a slice of Emmental and place the bun 'lids' on top. Serve immediately.

Makes 4

750g minced beef

3 tablespoons caramelised onion chutney (from a jar)

2 tablespoons balsamic glaze

6 tablespoons mayonnaise

3 teaspoons Tabasco sauce

Olive oil for brushing

4 burger buns

4 slices Emmental cheese

Salt and freshly ground black pepper

STEAK WITH CHILLI AND GARLIC ON ASPARAGUS *BISTECCA AGLIO E PEPERONCINO SU LETTO DI ASPARAGI*

I love a good steak, and it goes really well with asparagus. I use fillet steak for this recipe, which makes a lovely treat, but you could use a less expensive alternative, such as a minute steak cut from sirloin. You can also use green beans instead of asparagus. Always bring the steaks to room temperature before cooking. Serve with my Roasted new potatoes (see page 174).

1 Put the asparagus in a heatproof dish. Pour over enough boiling water to cover the spears. Set aside for 10 minutes then drain.

2 Using a sharp knife, cut the fillet into 12 equal-sized pieces. Gently push down each piece with the palm of your hand to flatten slightly. Set aside.

3 Put the oil, garlic and chilli in a large frying pan and place over a high heat. As soon as the garlic starts to sizzle, place the steaks in the pan and fry for 2 minutes each side (for medium). Sprinkle with salt. Using a fish slice, transfer the steaks to a warm plate and cover with foil. Return the pan to the heat.

4 Add the asparagus to the pan and fry for about 1 minute or until softened but still al dente. Sprinkle with salt.

5 Lift out the asparagus and divide it among 4 warm plates. Arrange 3 steaks, slightly overlapping, on top.

6 Pour the juices from the meat into the frying pan and stir to combine with the other ingredients. Drizzle the pan juices over the steaks and serve immediately.

Serves 4

250g fine asparagus spears, woody ends removed
1 piece centre-cut beef fillet (about 800g)
10 tablespoons extra virgin olive oil
5 large garlic cloves, peeled and thinly sliced
1 teaspoon dried chilli flakes
Salt

MEATBALLS IN A SPICY TOMATO SAUCE *POLPETTINE AL POMODORO*

I cooked these meatballs in Verona, after spending the afternoon as a life model for a group of artists … what an experience! The dish is incredibly quick, easy, really delicious and filling. I've used a combination of minced pork and beef, but if you prefer you can use minced lamb or ground chicken. Take the minced meat out of the fridge around 20 minutes before you cook the meatballs so they're not cold in the middle. If you don't like spice, simply leave out the chilli. Serve with plain boiled rice or warm crusty bread.

1 Place the pork, beef and caramelised onion chutney in a large bowl. Season with salt. Mix well with your hands until thoroughly combined. Take small amounts of the mixture and roll into 24 equal-sized balls (about the size of a golf ball). Set aside.

2 Heat the oil in a large, shallow saucepan or sauté pan over a medium heat. Add the meatballs and fry gently for about 8 minutes or until browned all over, turning carefully. Sprinkle over the chilli flakes and fry for a further 2 minutes, stirring occasionally.

3 Add the tomatoes and some salt. Simmer for about 10 minutes, then add the basil and cook for a further 15 minutes, stirring occasionally.

Serves 4

400g minced pork
400g minced beef
4 tablespoons caramelised onion chutney
6 tablespoons olive oil
2 teaspoons dried chilli flakes
2 x 400g tins of chopped tomatoes
10 fresh basil leaves
Salt

CALVES' LIVER IN A BUTTER AND SAGE SAUCE WITH TOASTED CIABATTA
FEGATO DI VITELLO AL BURRO E SALVIA CON CROSTINI

You can't get much more 'express' than this! If you've never tried calves' liver before, please do try this dish – it's so tasty, nutritious and easy. This is the traditional way of cooking liver in Italy – thinly sliced, sautéed quickly and with a butter and fresh sage sauce. The key things to remember are that the liver must be extremely fresh or it will have a grainy texture, and always take the meat out of the fridge 15 minutes before cooking. *Buon Appetito*!

1 Toast the ciabatta on both sides. Gently rub the garlic clove over both sides. Set aside.

2 Put the flour on a large plate and season with salt. Dip the liver in the seasoned flour to lightly coat. Shake off any excess flour and transfer to a plate.

3 Heat the oil, butter and sage in a large frying pan over a high heat. When hot, fry the liver in 2 batches for about 1 minute each side or until browned all over. Season with salt and pepper.

4 To serve, arrange 3 slices of liver on each warm plate and drizzle over the sage and butter sauce. Serve with the toasted ciabatta.

Serves 4

8 slices ciabatta bread, about 1cm thick
1 garlic clove, peeled
5 tablespoons plain flour
850g calves' liver, cut into 12 slices about 5mm thick
4 tablespoons olive oil
80g salted butter, cut into cubes
10 large fresh sage leaves
Salt and freshly ground black pepper

VEAL MILANESE *VITELLO ALLA MILANESE*

This is a Milanese classic and is one of my favourite ways to eat a veal chop. I prepared it for my friends in Treviglio, about 40 kilometres east of Milan, after a very long cycle ride around the town on the wonderful Bianchi bike I had borrowed from the factory where these iconic bikes are produced. Veal is traditional, but you can also make this recipe with chicken breasts, pork chops or lamb chops. Serve with a simply dressed salad.

1 Place the chops on a board. Using a sharp knife, scrape any skin from the outside of the bone until clean. Using a meat mallet, rolling pin or heavy-based pan, pound the veal to about 5mm thick. Make about 3 cuts in the fat to stop the meat from curling. Set aside.

2 Break the eggs into a large bowl and season with salt and pepper. Place the breadcrumbs on a large plate or tray.

3 Dip each chop in the breadcrumbs (shake off any excess), then in the eggs (make sure the meat and bone are completely immersed), then in the breadcrumbs again. Ensure each chop is evenly coated.

4 Place the chop on a board and press down the meat slightly using the palm of your hand.

5 Put the oil in a large frying pan, add the rosemary and garlic and place over a medium heat. To check if the oil is hot enough for frying, sprinkle some breadcrumbs into the oil; if the breadcrumbs start to sizzle, the oil is ready.

6 Fry the chops in 2 batches for 4 minutes each side or until light golden brown (if you prefer your meat more well done, fry for 1 minute longer each side). Drain on kitchen paper. Sprinkle over a little salt and serve with the lemon slices.

Serves 4

4 bone-in veal chops (about 200–250g each), trimmed
5 medium eggs
250g dried fine breadcrumbs
250ml olive oil
4 rosemary sprigs (about 10cm long)
4 garlic cloves, peeled
Lemon slices to serve
Salt and freshly ground black pepper

ITALIAN SAUSAGES AND BEANS WITH GARLIC CIABATTA *SALSICCE E FAGIOLI CON CROSTINI ALL'AGLIO*

When I was filming the latest TV series I cooked this hearty casserole with Lake Garda behind me, after spending all day with the local rowing team in the beautiful resort town of Sirmione. This dish says so much about rustic Italian cooking – simple ingredients that balance each other perfectly and punchy flavours. For variety, replace the beans with lentils or chickpeas.

1 Heat the oil in a large, heavy-based saucepan or flameproof casserole over a high heat. Add the onions, rosemary, chilli flakes and salt. Fry for about 12 minutes, stirring occasionally.

2 Meanwhile, drain any excess juices from the top of the beans. Do not drain completely, as the juices will help to create a smooth, thick sauce. Set aside.

3 Add the sausages to the pan and fry for 10 minutes, stirring every couple of minutes. Add the beans, stock and tomato purée, season with salt and bring to the boil.

4 Reduce the heat to medium and cook for 20 minutes (uncovered), stirring frequently. Remove from the heat, stir in the parsley and let rest for 10 minutes. Meanwhile, preheat a ridged cast-iron chargrill pan over a high heat for 5–10 minutes.

5 To make the garlic ciabatta, rub or brush a little oil on both sides of the bread. When the pan is very hot, lay the ciabatta in the pan and grill for about 1 minute each side or until dark golden brown. Rub the garlic clove over both sides of the toasts.

6 Divide the sausages and beans among warm bowls, sprinkle over the parsley and serve immediately with the garlic ciabatta.

Serves 4–6

6 tablespoons olive oil, plus extra for brushing
2 red onions, peeled and thinly sliced
1 tablespoon chopped fresh rosemary
½ teaspoon dried chilli flakes
2 x 400g tins of borlotti beans
2 x 400g tins of cannellini beans
900g Italian sausages or good-quality pork sausages, cut into pieces 4cm long
400ml hot vegetable stock
1 tablespoon tomato purée
3 tablespoons chopped fresh flat-leaf parsley, plus extra to garnish
1 ciabatta loaf, cut diagonally into slices 2cm thick
1 large garlic glove, peeled
Salt

SPICY WARM LAMB SALAD WITH ARTICHOKES AND WALNUTS

INSALATA CALDA DI AGNELLO PICCANTE CON CARCIOFI E NOCI

If you're looking for something a little bit unusual to serve at a dinner party, this is a great choice, as it never fails to impress. It looks stunning, and the juicy slices of lamb, artichokes and walnuts make an amazing combination of flavours and textures. The timings I have given are for quite rare meat; if you prefer medium, cook the fillets for about 3 minutes longer. Either way, take them out of the fridge about 20 minutes before cooking. Serve with warm crusty bread.

1 Place a large frying pan over a high heat for 2 minutes. Meanwhile, place the lamb fillets on a large plate and drizzle 2 tablespoons of the oil over each fillet. Rub the oil into the fillets on both sides until evenly coated and season with salt and pepper.

2 When the pan is very hot, lay the fillets in the pan and fry for about 7 minutes, turning halfway through cooking, or until brown on all sides. Transfer to a board, cover with foil and leave to rest for 3–5 minutes.

3 Return the pan to the heat. Add the artichokes, walnuts and chillies, then the balsamic glaze and the wine. Stir for about 30 seconds to combine. Remove from the heat.

4 To serve, carve the lamb into slices about 5mm thick. Arrange the meat, slightly overlapping, on 4 plates.

5 Spoon over the artichokes, walnuts and chillies, and any remaining juices from the pan. Arrange the rocket on top and drizzle over the remaining 4 tablespoons of oil. Sprinkle a little salt on top of the rocket leaves and serve immediately.

Serves 4

2 x 300g fillets of lamb
8 tablespoons extra virgin olive oil
280g chargrilled artichoke hearts in oil, drained and quartered
60g walnut halves
2 fresh, medium-hot red chillies, deseeded and finely sliced
4 tablespoons balsamic glaze
60ml dry white wine
60g rocket leaves
Salt and freshly ground black pepper

VEGETABLE FRITTATA WITH ASIAGO *FRITTATA CON PATATE, ASPARAGI, VERDURE E ASIAGO*

Containing a variety of vegetables, potatoes and cheese, this frittata is both filling and nutritious. It makes a perfect lunch or light supper and is also great for a packed lunch the following day. Asiago is a classic northern Italian cow's milk cheese made in Trentino-Alto Adige and Veneto, and it melts beautifully. It can be tricky to find, but fontina cheese, or a strong Cheddar, works well too. For maximum flavour, serve at room temperature.

1 Place the potatoes in a medium saucepan. Cover with hot water, add some salt and bring to the boil. Add the asparagus, broccoli and peas and boil for 5 minutes or until just tender. Drain and set aside.

2 Heat the oil in a 24cm heavy-based, non-stick frying pan over a medium heat. Add the spring onions and fry for about 3 minutes, stirring occasionally. Add the drained vegetables and the chives and fry for 2 minutes. Meanwhile, preheat the grill to a medium-high setting.

3 Season the beaten eggs with salt and pepper and pour them over the vegetables. Tilt the pan so the eggs cover the bottom of the pan evenly. Reduce the heat slightly and cook for 6–8 minutes. Do not stir; instead, move the pan around on the flame so the bottom does not burn.

4 Scatter over the Asiago and place the pan under the hot grill for 3–6 minutes or until the frittata is set and golden brown. If your frying pan has a plastic/rubber handle, cover with foil to prevent it from melting.

5 Remove from the grill and leave to rest in the pan for 2–5 minutes then turn out onto a serving plate. Leave to cool then cut into wedges.

Serves 6

400g baby potatoes, scrubbed and quartered

150g fine asparagus spears, woody ends removed and cut diagonally into 3cm lengths

100g broccoli, cut into small florets

100g frozen peas, defrosted

2 tablespoons olive oil

100g spring onions, trimmed and chopped

3 tablespoons chopped fresh chives

9 medium eggs, lightly beaten

100g Asiago cheese, cut into small pieces

Salt and freshly ground black pepper

EGGS POACHED IN MEDITERRANEAN VEGETABLE RAGÙ *SPEZZATINO DI VERDURE CON UOVA*

Throughout the Mediterranean, including North Africa and the Middle East, there are variations on the theme of eggs poached or baked in a tomato sauce. I like to include a variety of Mediterranean vegetables, as well as borlotti beans, to make it more substantial. This is a delicious, colourful dish for brunch, lunch or a light supper, and what's more it's all cooked in one pan, so very little washing up is needed. Serve with my Cheesy ciabatta (see page 62).

1 Heat the oil in a large shallow saucepan or sauté pan over a medium heat. Add the onion and fry for 5 minutes, stirring occasionally. Tip in the pepper and fry gently for about 8 minutes. Add the chilli flakes, aubergine and courgette, sprinkle over the salt and fry for 10 minutes, stirring occasionally.

2 Increase the heat. Stir in the tomatoes, beans and stock and bring to the boil. Reduce the heat to medium, add the parsley and simmer for 10 minutes or until you have a fairly thick sauce, stirring occasionally.

3 Reduce the heat to low. Using the back of a spoon, make 4 dips in the vegetable mixture. Carefully break an egg directly into each dip, being careful not to break the yolk. Cover the saucepan with a lid and simmer gently for about 7 minutes or until the whites are set but the yolks are still runny.

4 To serve, carefully transfer to warm bowls, allowing 1 egg per person. Sprinkle over the pecorino.

Serves 4

6 tablespoons olive oil
1 large red onion, peeled and thinly sliced
1 large yellow pepper, deseeded and sliced into strips 5mm thick
1 teaspoon dried chilli flakes
1 medium aubergine, cut into 1cm cubes
1 large courgette, halved lengthways then cut across into slices 5mm thick
2 x 400g tins of chopped tomatoes
1 x 400g tin of borlotti beans, rinsed and drained
100ml hot vegetable stock
2 tablespoons chopped fresh flat-leaf parsley
4 medium eggs
30g freshly grated pecorino cheese
Salt

S SALADS & SIDES

SALADS & SIDES S

RECIPES

MIXED BEAN, CHICKPEA AND CHERRY TOMATO SALAD *INSALATA DI FAGIOLI, CECI E POMODORINI*

This no-fuss salad can be served as a starter or as an accompaniment to fish or meat, and also makes a great packed lunch to take to work. It's quick to prepare, filling and very nutritious. You can easily adapt this recipe, adding or removing whatever you like. Sometimes I stir in a couple of tins of tuna in oil for variety. Serve with warm crusty bread or garlic ciabatta (see page 143).

1 Put the cannellini beans, butter beans and chickpeas in a sieve placed over the sink. Rinse under cold running water and drain. Rinse and drain the kidney beans separately. Leave them all to drain until completely dry.

2 Put the tomatoes, onion and drained beans and chickpeas in a large bowl. Stir in the lemon zest and juice.

3 Pour over the oil and stir gently to combine. Season with salt and pepper. Stir in the parsley and gently toss everything together.

Serves 6

1 x 400g tin of cannellini beans
1 x 400g tin of butter beans
1 x 400g tin of chickpeas
1 x 400g tin of red kidney beans
20 fresh red cherry tomatoes, halved
1 large red onion, peeled and finely chopped
Zest and juice of 2 unwaxed lemons
6 tablespoons extra virgin olive oil
3 tablespoons chopped fresh flat-leaf parsley
Salt and freshly ground black pepper

MAIN-DISH SALAD WITH HERB-CRUSTED HAM *INSALATA CON PROSCIUTTO COTTO*

Substantial enough to serve as a main course, this salad makes a great lunch or supper. In addition to ham it contains all kinds of goodies, including avocados, sweetcorn, sun-dried tomatoes and Parmesan. If you like, you could also add a few good-quality pitted green olives. You can find herb-crusted ham in many delis, where they can cut it thickly for you, but if you have no luck, buy any herb-crusted ham and slice it thinly.

1 Tear the lettuce into pieces and place in a large bowl. Add the rocket, ham, avocado, sweetcorn and semi-dried tomatoes. Sprinkle over half the pecorino.

2 To make the dressing, put the mustard, vinegar and 2 tablespoons of water in a small bowl. Gradually add the oil and whisk to create a smooth dressing. Season with salt and pepper.

3 Pour the dressing over the salad and gently toss to combine. Divide between 4 plates and sprinkle over the remaining pecorino.

Serves 4

1 iceberg lettuce
60g rocket leaves
300g herb-crusted cooked ham, sliced
  thickly and cut into 1cm cubes
1 ripe avocado, halved, stoned, peeled
  and cut into chunks
1 x 195g tin of sweetcorn, drained
100g semi-dried tomatoes in oil, drained
50g freshly grated pecorino cheese

For the dressing
½ teaspoon Dijon mustard
1 tablespoon white wine vinegar
5 tablespoons extra virgin olive oil
Salt and freshly ground black pepper

MEDITERRANEAN PASTA SALAD *INSALATA DI PASTA*

If you've never cooked before, this is a great recipe to start with, as very little can go wrong. Just make sure you cook the pasta until al dente – that is, firm with some bite – you don't want soggy pasta. I've suggested a list of ingredients, but you can add pretty much whatever you like – peas, artichokes, cooked ham or tins of sweetcorn and tuna all work well in a pasta salad.

1 Cook the farfalle in a large pan of boiling, salted water until al dente. Drain and rinse under cold running water for 3 minutes, moving the pasta around in the colander so it cools more quickly. Leave to drain thoroughly.

2 Put the farfalle in a large bowl. Add the oil and pesto, season with salt and pepper and stir to combine.

3 Add the mayonnaise, onion, tomatoes, olives, peppers and gherkins. Stir to combine. Add the mozzarella and half the Parmesan shavings. Toss well to mix and taste for seasoning.

4 Transfer the salad to a large serving platter. Scatter over the remaining Parmesan.

Serves 4

400g dried farfalle
6 tablespoons extra virgin olive oil
3 tablespoons basil pesto
5 tablespoons mayonnaise
1 large red onion, peeled and thinly sliced
15 fresh red cherry tomatoes, quartered
150g pitted black olives (preferably Leccino), drained and halved
1 red pepper, deseeded and finely diced
1 yellow pepper, deseeded and finely diced
100g pickled small gherkins, drained and finely diced
2 x 125g balls of mozzarella cheese, drained and cut into small cubes
80g Parmesan cheese shavings
Salt and freshly ground black pepper

ITALIAN RICE SALAD *INSALATA DI RISO*

When I was a little boy my mother, Alba, used to make this rice salad for my lunch box. It's a very useful recipe, as you can prepare the salad a day ahead, refrigerate it and take it to work the following day. For maximum flavour, it's best eaten at room temperature, rather than straight from the fridge.

1 Bring 2.5 litres of salted water to the boil in a medium saucepan. Add the rice and cook for about 12 minutes, stirring occasionally. Add the peas and beans and boil for 2 minutes.

2 Tip into a sieve placed over the sink. Rinse under cold running water for 1 minute to cool, then leave to drain thoroughly. Tip into a large mixing bowl.

3 Add all the remaining ingredients, except the boiled eggs and Parmesan, and stir gently until everything is well combined. Season with salt and pepper.

4 Transfer the rice salad to a large serving plate. Arrange the boiled eggs around the dish and scatter over the Parmesan.

Serves 6

300g long-grain rice
100g frozen peas, defrosted
100g green beans, cut into 2cm lengths
100g pitted green olives, drained and halved
100g small pickled gherkins, finely chopped
1 red pepper, deseeded and finely chopped
1 yellow pepper, deseeded and finely chopped
10 fresh red cherry tomatoes, quartered
5 tablespoons mayonnaise
5 tablespoons extra virgin olive oil
6–8 medium boiled eggs, peeled and quartered
50g Parmesan cheese shavings
Salt and freshly ground black pepper

MODENA-STYLE ROASTED ONIONS IN BALSAMIC VINEGAR
CIPOLLE BORETTANE

If you visit Modena, in the Emilia-Romagna region, you won't be able to miss these amazing onions, pickled in balsamic vinegar. They're also available in some UK supermarkets in jars (called Borettane onions). You can serve them as an antipasti, like olives, with a little warm crusty bread and a glass of Italian red wine. Alternatively, they are a good accompaniment to fish or meat dishes. A useful tip is to soak the onions or shallots in hot water for 2–3 minutes before you peel them. The skins will come off much more easily.

1 Preheat the oven to 180°C/gas mark 4. Heat the oil in a large frying pan over a medium heat. Add the onions and rosemary and fry for about 10 minutes, stirring frequently.

2 Add the vinegar, honey and 150ml of hot water. Season with salt and pepper. Simmer for about 10 minutes, stirring occasionally.

3 Transfer the onions to a medium roasting tin and roast for about 15 minutes or until soft, turning halfway through cooking.

Serves 6

5 tablespoons extra virgin olive oil
50 pickling onions or shallots (about 1kg), peeled
2 tablespoons fresh rosemary leaves
10 tablespoons balsamic vinegar
4 tablespoons runny honey
Salt and freshly ground black pepper

CARROTS IN WHITE WINE WITH MINT AND CHILLI *CAROTE AL VINO BIANCO, MENTA E PEPERONCINO*

Since I created this recipe, it's the only way we eat carrots at home – my family would never go back to boring boiled carrots. They're a great accompaniment to any fish or meat dishes, and the flavour of the wine with the fresh mint and chilli works to perfection. If I have any left over, I put them in a frittata the following day, or simply toss them into a salad.

1 Heat the butter and oil in a medium saucepan over a medium heat. Meanwhile, bruise the garlic by placing a clove under the flat side of a large knife and pressing down. When the butter has melted, add the garlic and chilli flakes and fry gently for 2 minutes, stirring continuously.

2 Add the carrots, sugar and some salt and fry gently for 2 minutes, stirring occasionally.

3 Increase the heat, pour in the wine and bring to the boil. Reduce the heat and simmer for 12 minutes, stirring occasionally, or until the carrots are cooked but still al dente.

4 Remove and discard the garlic. Stir in the fresh mint and serve immediately.

Serves 4

80g salted butter
2 tablespoons olive oil
2 large garlic cloves, peeled
1 teaspoon dried chilli flakes
500g carrots, peeled and cut into 5mm rounds
1 teaspoon caster sugar
150ml dry white wine
8 large mint leaves, finely sliced
Salt

ASPARAGUS WITH BUTTER AND PECORINO *ASPARAGI BURRO E PECORINO*

Italy is one of Europe's leading asparagus producers. Over half comes from Puglia, in southern Italy, but it is also grown in northern Italy, particularly in Veneto and Emilia-Romagna, but also around Pisa and Lucca, in Tuscany. Asparagus with melted butter is a classic combination, but what makes this dish special is the pecorino – an Italian cheese made from sheep's milk, with a sharp, salty flavour. If you can't find pecorino you can use Parmesan instead.

1 Bring a large saucepan of salted water to the boil over a high heat. Add the asparagus to the boiling water and simmer for 4 minutes or until just tender. Drain well.

2 Meanwhile, melt the butter in a small saucepan over a low heat.

3 Arrange the asparagus on a large serving platter or individual plates. Pour over the melted butter and season with salt and pepper. Sprinkle over the pecorino.

Serves 4

400g asparagus spears, woody ends removed
150g salted butter
80g freshly grated pecorino cheese
Salt and freshly ground black pepper

BAKED LAYERED POTATOES WITH MUSTARD AND PECORINO *PATATE AL FORNO CON SENAPE E PECORINO SARDO*

This recipe is dedicated to my great friend, the French maître d' Fred Sirieix. I have taken one of his favourite French dishes and added Italian flavours, and as he would say, '*Voilà*!' This is a fantastic dish for entertaining, as you can prepare it in the morning, then bake it later. Keep it in the fridge, covered, and make sure you take it out of the fridge at least 15 minutes before cooking.

1 Preheat the oven to 180°C/gas mark 4. Lightly butter a baking dish, about 24 x 20cm and 5cm deep.

2 Put the double cream in a medium saucepan, stir in the garlic and nutmeg and bring to the boil. Remove from the heat and stir in the mustard. Set aside.

3 Arrange a single layer of potatoes in the prepared baking dish (do not overlap). Dot small knobs of butter in each corner and season with salt and pepper. Continue layering the potatoes, butter and seasoning, until you have used all the potatoes or reached the top of the dish (there will be about 5 layers).

4 Carefully pour the cream mixture over the potatoes and cover with foil. Bake for 70 minutes. Remove the foil, top with 8 small knobs of butter and sprinkle over the pecorino. Return to the oven (uncovered) and cook for a further 30 minutes or until the potatoes are tender and the top golden brown.

5 Remove the dish from the oven and leave to rest for about 15 minutes before serving.

Serves 6

600ml double cream
2 garlic cloves, peeled and thinly sliced
3 teaspoons grated nutmeg
3 teaspoons Dijon mustard
6 large potatoes (about 1kg), peeled and
  thinly sliced
50g salted butter, cut into small knobs, plus
  extra for greasing
50g freshly grated pecorino cheese
Salt and freshly ground black pepper

ROASTED NEW POTATOES WITH PEPPERS, GARLIC AND ROSEMARY
PATATE ARROSTO CON PEPERONI, AGLIO E ROSMARINO

This is the way my mother used to cook potatoes for me when I was growing up, and it's how I make roast potatoes for my wife and children today. It's a really easy recipe, as everything goes into one roasting tin and there's no need to parboil the potatoes. If you prefer, you can use courgettes or carrots instead of peppers and fresh thyme instead of rosemary. It makes a perfect accompaniment to any fish or meat dish.

1 Preheat the oven to 200°C/gas mark 6. Put the potatoes, peppers, garlic and rosemary in a medium roasting tin. Pour over the oil and season with salt and pepper.

2 Toss the vegetables in the oil. Use your hands to combine all the ingredients and make sure everything is well coated in the oil, including the bottom of the tin.

3 Roast for 40 minutes or until the potatoes are tender and golden brown, stirring halfway through cooking. Serve immediately.

Serves 4

600g baby potatoes, scrubbed

1 large red pepper, deseeded and sliced into strips 5mm thick

1 large yellow pepper, deseeded and sliced into strips 5mm thick

1 large green pepper, deseeded and sliced into strips 5mm thick

4 garlic cloves (unpeeled)

2 tablespoons fresh rosemary leaves

6 tablespoons olive oil

Salt and freshly ground black pepper

TRADITIONAL ITALIAN FLATBREAD *PIADINE*

Piadine – a popular street food in Emilia-Romagna – are becoming very fashionable in the UK, perhaps because so many people are trying to avoid bread with yeast in it. You can either serve these flatbreads just as they are, while they're still warm, to accompany soups, dips, antipasti or a main course, or fill them as you would a wrap with whatever ingredients you fancy, including meat, vegetables or cheese.

1 Combine the flour, salt and pepper in a medium bowl. Make a well in the centre and gradually add 1 tablespoon of the oil and 110ml warm water. Mix together using the handle of a wooden spoon to form a soft, wet dough.

2 Gather the dough and knead on a lightly floured surface for 5–10 minutes or until smooth and elastic. Place the dough in a large oiled bowl, cover with cling film and leave to rest at room temperature for about 15 minutes.

3 Divide the dough into 4 equal-sized pieces and use a rolling pin to roll out each into a thin disc, about 18cm diameter. Cover with a tea towel until ready to cook. Lay a sheet of greaseproof paper on the work surface.

4 Heat the remaining 2 tablespoons of oil in a large frying pan over a medium heat until very hot (about 3 minutes). Add one of the piadine and fry for 1–2 minutes or until it starts to turn golden brown, then turn and fry for a further 1–2 minutes.

5 Transfer the piadina to the greaseproof paper. Lay a sheet of greaseproof paper on top and cover with a tea towel. Repeat for all the piadine, putting greaseproof paper between the layers and covering the pile with a tea towel to keep warm.

Makes 4

180g strong white flour, plus extra for dusting
1 teaspoon fine salt
½ teaspoon freshly ground black pepper
3 tablespoons extra virgin olive oil

SSERTS DESSERTS

DESSERTS DESSERT

RECIPES

QUICK LIMONCELLO ICE CREAM WITH MIXED BERRIES *GELATO VELOCE CON LIMONCELLO E FRUTTI DI BOSCO*

The *digestivo* limoncello, made from lemons, has been produced in Italy for centuries, particularly in the south, where the winters are milder. This limoncello and berry ice cream is the quickest ice cream you're ever likely to make. You can use any kind of frozen berries; I usually use cherries, strawberries, raspberries and blackcurrants. If you prefer, you can use freshly squeezed lemon juice or an orange liqueur, such as Cointreau, instead of limoncello. I sometimes like to drizzle runny honey over the top.

1 Put the frozen berries, limoncello, yogurt, honey and vanilla in a food processor. Blitz until smooth. Set aside.

2 Pour the cream into a medium bowl. Lightly whisk using a hand whisk until the cream is thick enough to just hold its shape and form soft peaks (about 4 minutes). Do not over whisk or the mixture will be too stiff.

3 Gently fold the puréed berry mixture into the whipped cream. Spoon the mixture into a 1-litre shallow, rigid freezerproof container. Cover and freeze for 2 hours.

4 Remove the ice cream from the freezer. Use a fork to scrape the partly frozen crystals from the edge and stir until the mixture is well blended and smooth. Return the container to the freezer for a further 2 hours or until set.

5 About 10 minutes before you are ready to serve, remove the ice cream from the freezer. Serve with some berries alongside.

Serves 8

500g frozen mixed berries, plus extra
  to serve
5 tablespoons limoncello (lemon liqueur)
200g Greek yogurt
6 tablespoons runny honey
1 tablespoon vanilla extract
300ml double cream

CHOCOLATE, HAZELNUT AND AMARETTO ICE CREAM *GELATO ALLA NUTELLA E AMARETTO*

This ice cream was inspired by my trip to Piedmont – the home of the world-famous hazelnut and chocolate spread, Nutella. At home I always make a double batch of it as, trust me – once your kids or guests try this dessert they will want more and more. You don't have to use amaretto (almond liqueur), but I like the combination of chocolate and almonds, so have included it in this recipe.

1 Put the egg yolks and sugar in a large heatproof bowl and set the bowl over a saucepan of simmering water. Ensure the base of the bowl is not touching the water. Whisk using an electric whisk for about 3–5 minutes or until the sugar has dissolved and the mixture is pale and thick.

2 Remove from the heat and whisk in the hazelnut chocolate spread. Leave to cool completely.

3 Pour the cream into a large bowl. Lightly whisk using a hand whisk until the cream is thick enough to just hold its shape and form soft peaks (about 5 minutes).

4 Using a flexible spatula, gently fold the whipped cream into the cooled hazelnut mixture in 3 stages. Fold in the hazelnuts and amaretto.

5 Spoon the mixture into a 1-litre shallow, rigid freezerproof container. Cover and freeze for at least 6 hours or until set, preferably overnight.

6 About 10 minutes before you are ready to serve, remove the ice cream from the freezer. Top each serving with chopped hazelnuts.

Serves 6-8

10 medium egg yolks
120g caster sugar
300g hazelnut chocolate spread
  (e.g. Nutella)
500ml double cream
100g roasted chopped hazelnuts,
  plus extra to decorate
6 tablespoons amaretto (almond liqueur)

STRAWBERRIES WITH LIMONCELLO, CHOCOLATE YOGURT AND HAZELNUTS COPPETTE DI FRAGOLE CON LIMONCELLO, YOGURT AL CIOCCOLATO E NOCCIOLINE

This delicious dessert combines two key ingredients that are always a hit with guests – strawberries and chocolate. It's a particularly useful recipe if you want to serve strawberries out of season, as the marinating in limoncello and honey really draws out their flavour. You can use freshly squeezed lemon juice instead of limoncello if you prefer.

1 Remove and discard the green stalks of the strawberries and cut the strawberries in half (or quarters if very large). Place in a large non-metallic bowl.

2 Pour over the limoncello and drizzle over the honey. Gently stir to combine. Leave to marinate for 10 minutes at room temperature, stirring occasionally.

3 Put the yogurt and chocolate in a small bowl and stir to combine. Divide between 4 dessert glasses. Spoon over the strawberries.

4 Drizzle with the remaining juices from the marinade and sprinkle over the hazelnuts. Dust with a little icing sugar and serve.

Serves 4

600g strawberries
3 tablespoons limoncello (lemon liqueur)
2 tablespoons runny honey
300g plain Greek yogurt
100g milk chocolate bar, chopped into
  small pieces (about the size of a pea)
2 tablespoons roasted chopped hazelnuts
Icing sugar, sifted, to decorate

LEMON TIRAMISÙ WITH LIMONCELLO *TIRAMISÙ AL LIMONE E LIMONCELLO*

Liguria is famous for its lemons, and I made this lovely light version of tiramisù for my friends Lise and Bartolo, who own a vineyard in the hills near the Cinque Terre town of Vernazza. I used lemons harvested from their back garden and their homemade limoncello, which was superb. This dessert really tastes of Italy, and it's great for entertaining as you can make it up to 12 hours ahead.

1 Put the egg whites in a large bowl and add half the sugar. Whisk with an electric whisk until they form stiff peaks.

2 Place the egg yolks in a large bowl and add the remaining sugar. Whisk for about 3 minutes or until thick and pale. Add the mascarpone and whisk to combine. Stir in the lemon zest. Using a flexible spatula or metal spoon, gently fold the egg whites into the mascarpone mixture. Set aside.

3 Pour 100ml cold water into a non-metallic dish and stir in the lemon juice and limoncello. Set aside.

4 Take 6 dessert glasses, about 8cm diameter and 8cm high. Spoon 2 tablespoons of the mascarpone mixture into each glass and spread to cover the bottom.

5 Dip a biscuit in the lemon water for no more than 2 seconds, cut the biscuit in half across and lay both halves, sugared-side up, on top of the mascarpone. Repeat for the remaining glasses.

6 Spread 2 further tablespoons of the mascarpone mixture over the biscuits, then cover with another layer of the remaining biscuits dipped in the lemon water and halved as previously. Top with a final layer of the mascarpone mixture. Cover with cling film and chill for about 5 hours or until set.

7 To serve, remove the cling film and grate over a little lemon zest.

Serves 6

4 medium eggs, separated
100g caster sugar
500g mascarpone cheese, drained
Zest and juice of 2 unwaxed lemons, plus extra lemon zest to decorate
4 tablespoons limoncello (lemon liqueur)
12 Savoiardi biscuits (sponge fingers)

AMARETTO CREAM WITH AMARETTI BISCUITS *CREMA DI AMARETTO CON AMARETTI*

I love the Italian almond liqueur amaretto – it has such an intense, sweet flavour and goes so well with most desserts, particularly those containing chocolate, fruit or cream. This recipe just couldn't be simpler or quicker. The amaretto is simply folded into double cream, which is then whipped and topped and tailed in a dessert glass with crushed amaretti biscuits for added almond flavour and crunch. I use 150ml martini glasses for this recipe.

1 Crush the amaretti biscuits, about 3 at a time, in your hand; you want a variety of different-sized pieces, large and small, to provide variety of texture. Put on a large plate and set aside.

2 Put the amaretto and sugar in a large bowl and whisk using an electric whisk until combined. Pour over the cream and continue to whisk lightly until the cream is just thick enough to hold its shape and form soft peaks. Do not over whisk or the cream will be too stiff.

3 To serve, place 2 tablespoons of the crushed biscuits in the bottom of each dessert glass. Spoon over the amaretto cream. To finish, sprinkle over the remaining biscuits.

Serves 4

16 crunchy amaretti biscuits
60ml amaretto (almond liqueur)
30g caster sugar
300ml double cream

PEARS POACHED IN RED WINE WITH VANILLA *PERE COTTE AL VINO E VANIGLIA*

When I visited Monte Isola, an island in the middle of Lake Iseo in northern Italy, I cooked these delicious poached pears for the local mayor, Fiore, and Andrea, the boat builder. I was thrilled to be able to cook right in the middle of the main town, Peschiera Maraglio, alongside the lake. This dessert is best served at room temperature or warm rather than piping hot. It's best to avoid really soft pears for this dish as they can lose their texture and fall apart when poached.

1 Peel the pears, leaving the stalks intact, and trim the base. Arrange upright in a small to medium saucepan (they should fit snugly in a single layer).

2 Pour over the wine and add the vanilla extract, vanilla pod (if using), sugar and cinnamon. Bring to the boil over a medium heat.

3 Reduce the heat to low, cover and simmer gently for 30 minutes, moving the pears around every 10 minutes or so.

4 Using a slotted spoon, lift out the pears and transfer to a large plate. Cover with foil and set aside.

5 Return the wine to a medium heat and boil for 30 minutes (uncovered) until reduced to a syrup consistency, stirring occasionally. Leave to cool. Remove the vanilla pod and cinnamon stick.

6 To serve, place a pear on a plate and drizzle over the wine syrup. Decorate with a vanilla pod if you like.

Serves 6

6 large pears
750ml bottle of full-bodied red wine
2 teaspoons vanilla extract
1 vanilla pod, plus extra for decoration
  (optional)
250g caster sugar
1 cinnamon stick, broken in half

ORANGE AND GRAND MARNIER MOUSSE *MOUSSE DI ARANCE E GRAND MARNIER*

I first came across this classic Italian dessert as I was filming in a little town near Pisa. I loved its simplicity and the fact that not many ingredients are needed to make such a masterpiece. The orange zest works really well with the orange liqueur (I used Grand Marnier, but you could use Cointreau instead if you prefer). It is a perfect dessert for entertaining, as you can prepare it in the morning and chill it for up to 8 hours until you're ready to serve.

1 Put the egg yolks and half the sugar in a large bowl and whisk using a hand whisk until the yolks are thick and pale. Whisk in the mascarpone, orange zest and orange liqueur until well combined.

2 Place the egg whites in another large bowl. Whisk with an electric whisk on full speed until they form stiff peaks. Whisk in the remaining sugar 1 tablespoon at a time.

3 Using a metal spoon or flexible spatula, gently fold one third of the egg whites into the mascarpone mixture until blended. Fold in the remaining egg whites in two stages.

4 Spoon the mixture into individual glasses, cover with cling film and chill for at least 2 hours or until set.

5 Decorate each mousse with a little grated orange zest before serving.

Serves 4–6

3 large eggs, separated
70g caster sugar
250g mascarpone cheese, drained
Zest of 1 large orange, plus extra zest
  to decorate
3 tablespoons orange liqueur (e.g.
  Grand Marnier)

LIMONCELLO BISCUITS *LIMONCETTI*

I made my super-easy limoncello biscuits when I went to visit my friend
Stefano, who runs a restaurant in a community centre in the city of Bergamo.
I was so inspired by the story of the place that I decided to help him for the day.
If you prefer, you can use orange liqueur (Grand Marnier or Cointreau) instead
of limoncello and orange zest instead of lemon zest.

1 Preheat the oven to 180°C/gas mark 4. Line a large baking sheet with baking parchment and lightly grease with butter.

2 Put the egg whites in a large bowl and whisk using an electric whisk until stiff peaks form. Add the sugar, then the almonds and the lemon zest, stirring between each addition. Pour in the limoncello and stir to make a smooth paste.

3 Place heaped teaspoons of the mixture onto the prepared tray, spaced about 3cm apart to allow room to spread (the mixture should make about 35 biscuits).

4 Bake for 15 minutes or until light golden brown. Leave until cool and firm then lightly dust with icing sugar.

Makes about 35

Salted butter, for greasing
4 medium egg whites
350g caster sugar
350g ground almonds
Grated zest of 3 unwaxed lemons
2 tablespoons limoncello (lemon liqueur)
Icing sugar, sifted, to decorate

NO-BAKE CHOCOLATE AND HAZELNUT CHEESECAKE *CHEESECAKE A FREDDO ALLA CREMA DI CIOCCOLATO E NOCCIOLINE*

This chocolate cheesecake is extremely easy to prepare, yet looks so impressive. I got my inspiration for the recipe when visiting the town of La Morra, near Cuneo, in Piedmont. I met a doctor called Roberto, who travels on horseback to visit his patients in their homes. After a long day of horse-riding, he told me that the area was famous for its hazelnut trees, so I decided to include hazelnuts in this recipe – and here you are!

1 To make the base, put the biscuits in a food processor and blitz to fine crumbs. Add the melted butter and blitz again.

2 Tip the buttery crumbs into a non-stick springform cake tin, 23cm diameter. Press the mixture evenly over the bottom using your fingers and/or the back of a tablespoon. Transfer to the fridge and chill while you make the filling.

3 To make the filling, put the cream cheese and icing sugar in a large bowl and whisk using an electric whisk on a low setting until smooth and creamy. Gradually add the chocolate spread, vanilla and cocoa and continue whisking until smooth.

4 Spoon the mixture over the biscuit base and spread the mixture evenly using the back of the spoon. Cover with cling film. Place the tin on a tray and chill for at least 6 hours.

5 Meanwhile, make the topping. Put the chocolate spread in a large heatproof bowl with the vanilla. Heat the cream in a small saucepan over a medium heat. As soon as the cream starts to simmer, pour it over the chocolate mixture and leave for 2 minutes. Slowly stir until smooth then leave to cool slightly.

6 Remove the cake from the fridge, take off the cling film and spoon over the chocolate topping. Smooth the surface with the back of a spoon. Cover again with the cling film and freeze for about 2 hours or until firm.

7 Loosen the cheesecake from the tin by running a kitchen knife or palette knife dipped in hot water around the inside of the tin. Sprinkle over the hazelnuts. Carefully remove the cheesecake from the tin, unlatching the springform and lifting off the sides, and cut into slices.

Serves 8

300g digestive biscuits
150g salted butter, melted

For the filling
700g full-fat cream cheese (room temperature)
50g icing sugar
400g chocolate spread
2 teaspoons vanilla extract
2 tablespoons cocoa powder, sieved

For the topping
200g chocolate spread
2 teaspoons vanilla extract
80ml double cream
80g toasted hazelnuts, chopped

MACCHIATO MOUSSE *MOUSSE DI CAFFÈ MACCHIATO*

This recipe is rich and delicious, and perfect for a dinner party as it's showy without much effort and you can make it up to 8 hours ahead. You can use dessert glasses, as here, or serve the mousse in espresso cups or large shot glasses (in which case the recipe will serve 8). If you prefer, you can use a good brandy instead of amaretto. Don't worry if you don't have an espresso machine, just use 2 teaspoons of instant coffee in 40ml hot water instead.

1 Break the chocolate into a large heatproof bowl. Add the marshmallows, butter, sugar, espresso and amaretto. Set the bowl over a pan of gently simmering water. The base of the bowl should not touch the water. Leave until just melted then remove the pan from the heat, stir and leave to cool.

2 Pour the cream into a medium bowl. Lightly whisk using a hand whisk until the cream is thick enough to hold its shape. Using a flexible spatula, gently fold the cream into the chocolate mixture.

3 Spoon the mixture into 6 individual glasses, cover with cling film and chill for at least 1 hour or until set.

4 Meanwhile, in a small bowl combine the crème fraîche, icing sugar and vanilla.

5 To serve, spoon 1 large heaped tablespoon of the crème fraîche mixture on top of each mousse and spread evenly. Scatter 3 chocolate-covered coffee beans over the top of each.

Serves 6

150g dark chocolate (70% cocoa solids)
150g mini marshmallows
50g salted butter, cut into small cubes
50g caster sugar
40ml strong espresso coffee
40ml amaretto (almond liqueur)
300ml double cream
300ml crème fraîche
2 tablespoons icing sugar
1 teaspoon vanilla extract
18 chocolate-covered coffee beans
 to decorate

GINO'S PANFORTE *PANFORTE DI GINO*

For centuries the Tuscan towns of Siena and Asciano have claimed that they both invented panforte – an argument that has yet to be resolved. So, I've decided to settle the argument my way, and I will call this delicious dessert *Gino's* panforte – yes, it's now *my* recipe. Think of this dessert as the Italian version of the Christmas pudding. You can add different nuts if you prefer and can use amaretto (almond liqueur) instead of orange liqueur.

1 Grease a deep, loose-bottomed round cake tin, 23cm diameter, with oil and line with cling film. Set aside.

2 Break the chocolate into a large heatproof bowl and set the bowl over a pan of gently simmering water. The base of the bowl should not touch the water. Leave until just melted. Remove the pan from the heat, stir and leave the chocolate to cool slightly. Alternatively, melt the mixture in the microwave on high in short bursts, stirring in between.

3 Put the egg whites in another large bowl and whisk using a balloon whisk until frothy – stop before they form stiff peaks. Pour in the maple syrup and whisk again.

4 Using a metal spoon or flexible spatula, gently fold in the ground almonds to form a paste, then the remaining nuts, the candied peel, Cointreau and spices. Finally, fold in the melted chocolate.

5 Pour the mixture into the prepared tin, cover with cling film and chill for at least 3 hours or until set.

6 Turn out onto a serving plate, remove the cling film and dust with icing sugar.

Serves 8–10

Oil for greasing
310g dark chocolate (40% cocoa solids)
4 large egg whites
4 tablespoons maple syrup
225g ground almonds
75g raw blanched hazelnuts
70g walnut halves
70g whole blanched almonds
75g candied peel, roughly chopped
4 tablespoons orange liqueur (e.g. Cointreau)
½ teaspoon ground cinnamon
¼ teaspoon ground cloves
¼ teaspoon ground nutmeg
½ teaspoon ground black pepper
Icing sugar, sifted, for dusting

CHOCOLATE RICE POTS WITH RASPBERRIES, HONEY AND ALMONDS

RISOTTINO AL CIOCCOLATO, LAMPONI, MIELE E MANDORLE

When I visited the main rice-growing area of Italy, in the Po Valley, I went to the little town of Villimpenta, in Lombardy, where a risotto festival is held each year in June. I cooked my creamy chocolate risotto for about a hundred people, with the help of local chefs. I have to say, at the beginning the visitors were all a little unsure about my sweet risotto, as they had never tried it before, but when they tasted it, they loved it.

1 Put the milk, sugar and cocoa in a small saucepan and place over a low heat. Stir for 5 minutes until the sugar has dissolved.

2 Add the rice and stir. Increase the heat, bring to the boil and then immediately reduce the heat to low. Simmer gently for 30 minutes (uncovered), stirring occasionally.

3 Once the mixture has a thick, creamy texture and the rice is tender, stir in the butter, vanilla, honey and raspberries. Leave to rest for 1 minute off the heat.

4 Spoon the rice into cappuccino cups. Arrange 3 raspberries on top of each and scatter over the almonds. Serve immediately.

Serves 4

1 litre full-fat milk

40g caster sugar

4 teaspoons good-quality cocoa powder

200g Arborio rice

60g salted butter

4 teaspoons vanilla extract

4 tablespoons runny honey

200g fresh raspberries, plus 12 extra to decorate

2 tablespoons flaked almonds

D'ACAMPO FAMILY BANANA AND CHOCOLATE PANCAKES *PANCAKES CON BANANA E SALSA DI CIOCCOLATO*

In the D'Acampo family we have pancakes with banana and chocolate sauce for breakfast every Sunday, no matter what. It's simply not Sunday if we don't (well, that's what my kids say anyway!) For variety, you can use strawberries or apples instead of bananas and hazelnuts rather than flaked almonds.

1 Put the eggs in a medium bowl and gradually whisk in the flour using a hand whisk. Add 3 tablespoons of the milk and a pinch of salt and whisk again to create a smooth, creamy batter. Set aside.

2 Put the chocolate spread in a small saucepan and pour over the remaining 4 tablespoons of milk. Place the saucepan over a low heat and gently stir until the chocolate melts completely and becomes the consistency of double cream. Keep warm.

3 Heat a knob of butter in a small, non-stick frying pan (about 21cm diameter) over a low to medium heat. Add a quarter of the batter to the pan, tilting it to coat the bottom evenly. Fry for about 45–60 seconds, then turn the pancake over and cook the other side for about 30 seconds. Slide the pancake out onto a warm plate.

4 Repeat to make 3 more pancakes. Stack the pancakes on top of each other as soon as they are cooked (they will not stick together). Cover with a tea towel to keep warm.

5 To serve, place a pancake on a plate. Scatter over some banana slices and pour over the chocolate sauce. Sprinkle over the hazelnuts.

Makes 4

3 medium eggs
3 tablespoons plain flour
7 tablespoons full-fat milk
Pinch of salt
3 tablespoons chocolate spread
25g salted butter
3 bananas, peeled and sliced into rounds 1cm thick
2 tablespoons roasted chopped hazelnuts

FLOURLESS CHOCOLATE CAKE WITH MASCARPONE CREAM *TORTA SENZA FARINA AL CIOCCOLATO CON CREMA AL MASCARPONE*

You don't need to be gluten free to love this flourless chocolate cake. It has a wonderful rich, chocolatey flavour and a dense, fudgy texture, making it definitely more of a dessert than a cake. My wife, Jessica, often makes this at home as it's a winner every time. A dollop of mascarpone cream adds the perfect finishing touch.

1 Preheat the oven to 180°C/gas mark 4. Grease a deep, loose-bottomed round cake tin, 23cm diameter, with butter and line with baking parchment.

2 Break the chocolate into a large heatproof bowl, add the butter and set the bowl over a pan of gently simmering water. The base of the bowl should not touch the water. Leave until just melted. Remove the pan from the heat, stir and leave the chocolate to cool slightly. Alternatively, melt the mixture in the microwave on high in short bursts, stirring in between.

3 Put the egg yolks and icing sugar in another large bowl and whisk using a hand whisk or until fluffy and pale.

4 Put the egg whites in a medium bowl and whisk using an electric whisk on full speed until they form stiff peaks.

5 Fold the melted chocolate into the egg-yolk mixture until thoroughly combined. Stir in the hazelnuts, almonds and amaretto. Gently fold in the whites in 3 batches, using a metal spoon or flexible spatula.

6 Pour the mixture into the prepared tin and spread evenly. Bake for 25 minutes or until risen and shrinking away from the sides of the tin. Leave to cool in the tin for 15 minutes, then turn out onto a serving plate.

7 To make the mascarpone cream, put the mascarpone in a small bowl. Stir in the icing sugar and vanilla until well combined. Serve alongside the cake.

Serves 8

100g salted butter, plus extra for greasing
300g good-quality dark chocolate (70% cocoa solids)
4 large eggs, separated
150g icing sugar, sifted
80g chopped hazelnuts
150g ground almonds
4 tablespoons amaretto (almond liqueur)

For the mascarpone cream
250g mascarpone cheese, drained
1 tablespoon icing sugar, sifted
2 teaspoons vanilla extract

SUPER-EASY CHOCOLATE SOUFFLÉS WITH RASPBERRY SAUCE
SOUFFLÉ AL CIOCCOLATO CON COULIS DI LAMPONI

Yes it's a soufflé recipe, but please don't panic! These aren't like any other soufflés – they're super easy to make and you really can't go wrong. The quantities given here are for quite large soufflés, as I love them so much, but if you're serving them at the end of a large meal, you might prefer to make them in slightly smaller ramekins (around 250ml/300ml capacity), in which case they take slightly less time to cook (about 14–16 minutes) and serve 6.

1 First make the sauce. Blitz the raspberries in a food processor or blender then pass through a sieve into a small saucepan. Add the icing sugar and orange liqueur. Bring to a simmer over a low heat and cook for 3 minutes or until slightly reduced, stirring occasionally. Set aside and leave to cool.

2 Grease 4 tall ramekins, about 10cm diameter and 7cm high, with the butter. Sprinkle the inside with a little caster sugar and shake off any excess. Chill until required. Preheat the oven to 220°C/gas mark 7.

3 Break the chocolate into a medium heatproof bowl and set the bowl over a pan of simmering water. The base of the bowl should not touch the water. Once the chocolate has melted, whisk in the egg yolks, one at a time, until the mixture thickens. Remove from the heat.

4 Put the egg whites in a large bowl. Whisk with an electric hand whisk on full speed until they form stiff peaks. Add the caster sugar, 1 tablespoon at a time. Fold about 1 tablespoon of the egg whites into the melted chocolate, then fold the chocolate mixture into the remaining egg whites.

5 Divide the mixture among the prepared ramekins. Level the tops then run your finger inside the rim of each ramekin to remove any excess mixture (this will help the soufflé to rise evenly). Place the ramekins on a baking sheet and bake for about 15–18 minutes or until well risen and just wobbly in the middle.

6 To serve, dust the soufflés with icing sugar and top with a large tablespoon of mascarpone. Drizzle over the raspberry sauce and serve immediately.

Serves 4

20g salted butter (room temperature)
120g caster sugar, plus extra for lining the ramekins
300g dark chocolate (70% cocoa solids)
4 medium egg yolks
8 medium egg whites
Icing sugar, sifted, to decorate
150g mascarpone cheese, drained

For the sauce
150g raspberries
30g icing sugar
40ml orange liqueur (preferably Cointreau)

SUGAR-COATED BREAD WITH CINNAMON AND VANILLA *PANE ZUCCHERATO CON CANNELLA E VANIGLIA*

This quick and easy recipe is the perfect way to start or end the day, or anything in between. I use sliced white bread, but you can also use country-style bread. My grandmother, Flora, used to make this dish with stale bread, and it worked beautifully. For a special treat, serve this with my Chocolate, hazelnut and amaretto ice cream (see page 184).

1 Break the eggs into a large, shallow dish. Add the milk, vanilla and cinnamon and beat together using a hand whisk or fork.

2 Put the bread in the egg mixture. Leave to soak for 2 minutes each side. Meanwhile, put the sugar on a large plate or tray.

3 Heat the butter and oil in a large frying pan over a high heat. As soon as the butter starts to sizzle, add the bread and fry for about 2 minutes, then turn over and fry the other side for about 1 minute or until golden brown. Dip both sides of the bread in the sugar and serve immediately.

Serves 4

4 medium eggs
120ml full-fat milk
2 teaspoons vanilla extract
¼ teaspoon ground cinnamon
4 slices of white bread, cut in half
  diagonally
100g caster sugar
60g salted butter
2 tablespoons vegetable oil

UPSIDE DOWN APPLE CRUMBLE

This recipe doesn't have an Italian title and the reason is very simple – we don't have a recipe for apple crumble. My inspiration for this dish came as I was filming in Soprabolzano, in the northernmost region of Alto Adige (South Tyrol), close to Bolzano and overlooking the Dolomites. The locals eat a lot of apples, so I thought I would cook an English recipe with an Italian twist, using amaretti biscuits and amaretto liqueur, although you can use port or sherry if you prefer.

1 Heat the butter in a large frying pan over a medium heat. As soon as it starts to foam, add the apples and cinnamon and cook for 2 minutes, turning the apples so they are evenly coated in the butter.

2 Sprinkle over the sugar and cook gently for a further 6 minutes, turning every 2 minutes so the apples caramelise all over. Remove from the heat and set aside.

3 To make the crumble base, roughly crush all the biscuits into chunky pieces (you can use your hands and the pieces can vary in size). Put them in a bowl and pour over the honey. Using 2 tablespoons, stir to coat the biscuits in the honey (they will stick together).

4 Divide the biscuit mixture between 4 plates and spread out to make a disc about 10cm across. Put the plates in the fridge while you finish the apples.

5 Place the frying pan with the apples over a high heat for about 30 seconds. Remove the pan from the heat and pour over the amaretto. If you have a gas hob, return the pan to the heat and tilt the pan towards the flame so it will catch fire (keep one hand on the handle, but make sure your body and head are well away from the pan). Burn off the alcohol for about 10 seconds or until the flame goes out. Shake the pan for about 20 seconds. If you have an electric hob, use a barbecue lighter to light the alcohol vapours off the heat, then return the pan to the heat and continue as above.

6 Remove the plates from the fridge and spoon the apples over the crumble. Drizzle over the pan juices.

7 Spoon the mascarpone on top of the apples and sprinkle over a pinch of cinnamon. Serve immediately.

Serves 4

50g salted butter

3 large eating apples, peeled, cored and cut into 6 wedges

½ teaspoon ground cinnamon, plus extra to decorate

2 tablespoons soft brown sugar

12 crunchy amaretti biscuits (about 50g in total)

7 digestive biscuits (about 100g in total)

4 tablespoons runny honey

4 tablespoons amaretto (almond liqueur)

100g mascarpone cheese, drained

INDEX

Note: The recipes that appear in the TV series *Gino's Italian Express* are indicated with an asterisk*. Page numbers in *italics* refer to illustrations.

First published in Great Britain in 2019 by
Hodder & Stoughton
An Hachette UK company

1

Map illustration by Jedrzej Nyka © Hodder
& Stoughton, 2019

A CIP catalogue record for this title is
available from the British Library.

Hardback ISBN 978 1 529 35225 2
eBook ISBN 978 1 529 35226 9

Editorial Director: Nicky Ross
Project Editor: Polly Boyd
Design: Georgia Vaux
Photography: Dan Jones
Food Stylists: Claire Bassano,
Matthew Ford and Jenna Leiter
Props Stylist: Tonia Shuttleworth

Colour origination by Born Group
Printed and bound by Firmengruppe APPL,
aprinta druck, Wemding, Germany

Hodder & Stoughton policy is to use papers
that are natural, renewable and recyclable
products and made from wood grown in
sustainable forests. The logging and
manufacturing processes are expected to
conform to the environmental regulations
of the country of origin.

Hodder & Stoughton Ltd
Carmelite House
50 Victoria Embankment
London
EC4Y 0DZ
www.hodder.co.uk